foreword by **Dan Kimball**
author of *They Like Jesus but Not the Church*

# TEACHING
# THROUGH
# THE ART OF
# STORYTELLING

Creating Fictional Stories that
Illuminate the Message of Jesus

## Jon Huckins

 youth
specialties

ZONDERVAN.com/
**AUTHORTRACKER**
*follow your favorite authors*

ZONDERVAN

*Teaching Through the Art of Storytelling*
Copyright © 2011 by Jon Huckins

YS Youth Specialties is a trademark of YOUTHWORKS!, INCORPORATED and is registered with the United States Patent and Trademark Office.

This title is also available as a Zondervan ebook.
Visit www.zondervan.com/ebooks.

Requests for information should be addressed to:

Zondervan, *Grand Rapids, Michigan 49530*

ISBN 978-0-310-49409-6 (softcover)

Mason Jennings lyrics used by permission.

*Cover design: SharpSeven Design*
*Interior design: SharpSeven Design*

*Printed in the United States of America*

# CONTENTS

# DEDICATION

I dedicate this book to my first child, Haven. I never had the opportunity to meet you, but you allowed me to experience love in a way more profound than I had ever otherwise known. Your mother and I are proud of you and look forward to the day we meet you when all is restored.

# ACKNOWLEDGMENTS

This book has come to fruition because of endless support from those who've gone before and come alongside me. From editing to phone calls to encouragement to creating the experiences that this book revolves around, I'm extremely grateful for the collaborative effort this has been.

Special thanks to: Tony Jones, Tic Long, Dr. Daniel Kirk, Brian Barnes, Doug Huckins, Nate Millheim, Mark Scandrette, Chris Folmsbee, Ryan McRae, Mark Simmons, Steve Boutry, Larry Mylander, Michael York, Jesse Rice, Chip Johnson, Bob Reehm, Mark Miller, Jay Howver, Roni Meek, Dave Urbanski, Jon Hall, Dan Kimball, Mark Bruszer, Tom Bentley, Adam McLane, the crew at Creative Fuel Studios, and all of my teenage friends at Harbor Chapel Community Church who created a place for this form of storytelling to take shape.

Most of all, thanks to my wife Jan and daughter Ruby for the endless support, constructive criticism, and for allowing me to spend endless hours writing and rewriting this book.

# FOREWORD

So often we as youth leaders believe that if we just present the facts straight from the Scriptures, then our youth will learn and change.

Or if we just properly exegete the verses we teach, then our youth will change and follow the guidance of Scripture more closely.

Or if we just have enough funny openers, then our youth will learn our lessons better.

Or perhaps if we just offer nifty, fill-in-the-blank handouts with our main points (starting with the same letter, of course), then we will see youth advance in their walks with God.

Or maybe if our PowerPoint presentations are slick and full of cool graphics, then they'll become the keys to unlock the power of our teaching.

Or maybe it's our worship bands we need to focus on; perhaps if the music sets just the right tone and mood before we get up to speak, then youth will be inspired to love as the Scriptures command.

Many of these ideas and tools are helpful in teaching the Bible. But we can get so caught up and focused on them and other micro-methods that we miss what may be the most effective teaching tool (apart from prayer): teaching the full Bible "story" so that youth understand how and why all of its smaller stories fit together.

Without a handle on the full Bible story, ultimately much of what we teach youth about Scripture becomes confusing. Maybe not at first, but as they enter their college years and begin thinking and reasoning in more multilayered, holistic terms about faith and life, the many isolated, out-of-context Scripture accounts and teachings they were exposed to as teens just don't make sense anymore.

Only when we offer the full Bible story to teens—and especially their roles as characters within its still-unfolding narrative—will they fully grasp the power of Scripture.

That's why I was thrilled to read Jon Huckins' book on teaching through the art of storytelling. Perhaps you'll find yourself relating to Jon as he tells some of his own story—especially how he grew dissatisfied with the way he was viewing and taught the Bible early in his ministry.

I didn't grow up in church, but I can say that my experience entering the world of church was very much like Jon's: I was taught isolated verses—but not always their contexts in relation to their passages; I was offered object lessons from parables—but not how those parables fit into the larger series of parables they're part of. Nor was I clued into the larger meaning of the corresponding Bible chapters or books—or how the books fit within the whole story of the Bible.

Teaching the Bible through the art of storytelling is, in fact, how the Bible was originally taught—and that's what Jon wants from us: to become master storytellers like first-century rabbis and create our own modern-day parables.

What I found fascinating about this book is that I assumed I'd encounter nothing but ideas for teaching youth; but I found myself wrapped up in its pages and receiving a personal learning experience as well. It isn't just a collection of theories either; Jon also relates incredibly helpful real-life examples and illustrations that will stretch and challenge you as you adapt them to your own youth ministry.

I'm thankful for this book—it's a rarity in youth ministry, as it has the potential of impacting not only youth but also their youth leaders.

May you enjoy the story within.

Dan Kimball, author,
*They Like Jesus but Not the Church*,
www.dankimball.com

# INTRODUCTION
### "Is It Story Time?": Why I Wrote This Book
### (and How I Hope It Benefits You)

"Is it story time?" asked a sophomore girl who'd been participating in our community for the past year. I can honestly say she said it in an excited and anticipatory way. In fact she was waiting for the hang-out time and other activities to end so she could get to her favorite time of the night—story time.

Now, if your experience is anything like mine (primarily as a youth pastor), then you've probably noticed that the post-meal or snacks/hang-out/activity time is when most kids are ready to leave—or begin brainstorming about the significance of the life cycle of the butterfly. They may think, *the fun is over, now we have to pay our penance for the free food and activities.* Others may not see the teaching time as penance, but because they've been around so long, they're numb to the hopeful and inviting message of Jesus. While I know these dynamics are not true for everyone, my hope and prayer is that some of the experiences, stories, history, and resources you find in this book may lead you to a place where your teenagers are anxiously waiting and ready to engage in the powerful story of Jesus.

## The Goal of This Book

I want to offer this book as a resource to any verbal communicator who believes that story is an essential element in effective teaching. The goal of this book is to offer practical guidance on *why* teaching through the art of storytelling is so effective both theologically and philosophically. In addition, its goal is to offer guidance regarding *how* to create artful, primarily fictional stories that convey messages.

With that in mind, you can take or leave whatever content you choose. I believe this text has the potential to be more helpful if read in its entirety. But if you just want to steal a story or two, I have no problem with that at all.

## A Quick Storytelling Outline (from My Perspective)

Because each chapter refers to the storytelling process, I'm offering the following explanatory outline to give a picture (based only on my experience) of what I'm referring to. I'll get into more detail about what that looks like in later chapters. But for the sake of clarity and understanding, I thought I'd offer a quick example.

For the most part, the storytelling that I discuss involves:

- Story: A fictional, artful narrative with a setting, characters, and plot
- Goal: Presenting a topic that will lead to active conversation and positive life change
- Format: Each week about twenty minutes of the story is presented, followed by twenty to thirty minutes of discussion or conversation. Then during the following week, the story is continued, along with further discussion, until the story is completed. I've created some stories that have lasted two weeks and others up to five weeks.

That's *very* basic, but hopefully it gives you a snapshot of what we're discussing in the theological and philosophical sections of the book (Parts One and Two).

## Reading Recommendations

As you read through this book, you'll notice that I refer to many different texts and books that have been formative in my faith exploration and my development as a storyteller. They've not only offered insights into how to tell a story in an intentional way, but also taught me a great deal about why storytelling is important from a theological and philosophical standpoint. Again, with the intention of simply offering this book as a resource to fellow communicators, I view reading recommendations as a very helpful aspect (and hope you take advantage of them by reading them yourself).

## "Youth" Semantics

A term commonly used to describe a group of teenagers who regularly gather and experience life together is *youth group*. I know for most people it's simply a matter of semantics, but when I hear someone describe a dynamic group of teenagers as a "youth group," I'm left unsatisfied. As you read through this book, you'll notice that I use a variety of *creative* words to describe the kind of "youth group" that I have the honor of shepherding. Some of the words used to describe this contemplative, radical, spiritually growing, formative collection of individuals who are seeking to live life in the way of Jesus include *gathering*, *community*, and so on.

## My Hope

I didn't write this book because I consider myself further along in my faith than you or that I have "it" all figured out. Instead I hope that on every page, you'll sense a spirit of humility that I try so hard to live out on a daily basis. On my worst day I falter in this area; but on my best, I can truly say that I write these words only because I believe teaching through the art of storytelling is a useful tool in pointing us all toward a life lived as participants in the kingdom of God.

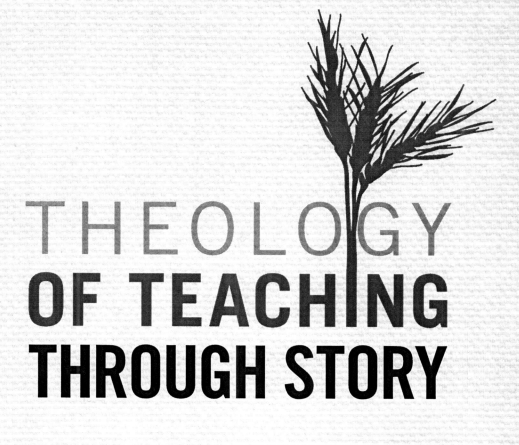

# THEOLOGY
# OF TEACHING
# THROUGH STORY

# 1

# UNDERSTANDING THE BIBLE AS A STORY WE CAN BE (ARE) A PART OF

"The significance (and ultimately the quality) of the work we do is determined by our understanding of the story in which we are taking part."

—Wendell Berry
www.crosscurrents.org/berry.htm

As we explore the theology of teaching through storytelling, we're beginning to see that much of the way Jesus taught and the forms in which he learned took place within the context of story. This understanding is paramount to our foundation as communicators who teach through the art of storytelling. And while it's important that we understand the context of Jesus' teaching and learning, it's equally important for each of us to come to our own understanding of the Bible—in its original context and free from our presuppositions.

To some degree we each have differing theologies based on our backgrounds, our personal understandings, and our overall view of God and faith in Jesus. Many would probably even disagree with my last point, saying, "My theological doctrine is written down and clearly explained in my denominational statement of faith" (or some other generally accepted foundational list). And to some degree I believe those articles are very important for us as we partner in our faith and move forward in a common, basic understanding of what we hold as truth. But I also believe we must acknowledge that we each look through different lenses of experience and understanding regarding the themes of Scripture based on our personal revelations and formative conversations and interactions.

One of my main intentions for beginning to teach through the art of storytelling was to create an atmosphere of a conversational, growing, and Spirit-led encounter with the Scriptures and our roles as individuals within that story.

## Sea-Lion Diaries

I'm very grateful for my upbringing, and many people—my parents, in large part—have encouraged me toward a faith that was real and growing. In many ways, their examples have been and continue to be a living and breathing picture of the life that Jesus intended for his people. That said, it's been essential for my development as a sincere follower of the Way to take an objective inventory of my theology and practice that's so easy to accept as the only articulation of Christian faith.

While I was growing up, my basic understanding of Scripture was that the Bible is a road map or user's manual for the Christian faith. There are some individual stories within the manual that taught me, but I had a hard time seeing a connection between those individual stories. This mentality led me to a faith that was confusing, frustrating, and extremely unsettling at times. The older I grew and the more I looked at each story within the Bible as a stand-alone lesson, the harder it became for me to understand some of the ways this book was supposed to lead people to a God of justice, compassion, grace, love, judgment, and ultimately relationship. It was as though I had a bunch of puzzle pieces that showed little bits of the larger picture, but they didn't make any sense on their own.

What led to even greater frustration were those television evangelists with their hair-sprayed silver locks who kept showing up on my local stations. They'd use one verse to explain why I needed to give them a certain dollar amount in order to receive the wealth and happiness that God had intended for us all. Or they mutilated a verse and claimed the Apocalypse was only six short years away, so I'd better turn to the "god" they described, or else I'd better put on my fire suit and lava boots. This skewed interpretation can lead to a posture of fear and condemnation rather than hope and invitation into the redemptive Story of God.

I didn't want to buy into their sales pitches, but I also didn't know of another way to look at the Bible that would explain this disconnect between what I believed to be true of God and what these people were telling me about God.

Thankfully, as I grew into my late teens and early twenties, I was surrounded by individuals who gave me room to start putting some of the puzzle pieces together. And that's how I received a much more comprehensive and holistic view of the Bible and its teachings. Toward the end of my high school years, I was blessed to have a youth pastor named Chip. (Isn't that every youth pastor's name?) He was a very gifted storyteller. We'd hear about his adventures skateboarding down Seattle streets or his near-death voyages among killer sea lions in a canoe he called "The Battle Ax."

Somehow—and I know many of us can relate—Chip was able to tie these ridiculous stories into beautiful and challenging pictures of what life could look like in the way of Jesus. The more I talked and shared life with him, the more I realized that his understanding of story didn't end with skateboarding, but it paralleled a larger biblical story. And I wanted to know more about this story.

So with Chip's mentorship and challenge, I began my quest for a more holistic picture of the Bible and its endless connection to story. I found that the Bible is filled with both fiction and nonfiction stories that use literary devices such at humor, syntax, rhetoric, character parallels, and irony—and the list goes on and on. In addition—and what I consider my most important discovery—I came to realize that all of the stories were somehow *connected*. Somehow all of the pieces came together to create this beautiful, profound, artful—and whole—mosaic. One may even call it a *masterpiece*. All these stories were part of a *bigger* story, and I wanted to be a part of it. But could I? Didn't the story end when John finished writing the book of Revelation? I needed to find out.

## Why So Many Divisions?

The more I looked and the more information I found, the more excited and engaged I became. Maybe the Bible was more than just a "road map for life" as I'd learned in Sunday school. Maybe my hair-sprayed friends on TV weren't telling the whole story. Maybe there was another way of looking at this book with which I'd become so disenchanted. I soon discovered that it wasn't the Bible that had disenchanted me; it was the incomplete way I'd learned to apply it to my life.

I learned that the current translations of the Bible, which I'd studied for so many years, might not have been organized in a way that made sense to

TEACHING THROUGH THE ART OF STORYTELLING

the authors of the day. For example, I found that the writings of Paul were, in large part, placed in order from longest to shortest book or letter: Is that how Paul would have wanted them arranged? Did such an order accurately reflect the real-life story that Paul was working so hard to tell?

Later I discovered that the chapter divisions in New Testament books weren't employed until the year 1205, and verse divisions weren't added until the 1550s (*The Books of the Bible*). Sometimes chapter divisions prevent complete thoughts and, conversely, force much smaller discussions within the context of one chapter. Is that how the chapters were intended to be read?

In regard to the verses, when they're treated as stand-alone units, they tend to encourage us to read the Bible as a reference book or road map (as I'd been taught while growing up). This leaves room for verses that are part of a bigger story to be taken out of context and distorted—much like what I'd observed on TV with "Hair Spray Guy." (*The Books of the Bible*, preface, v) If studied or read with the wrong understanding, these divisions could be toxic to understanding the larger biblical story.

## Biblical Story

Like many, one of my biggest theological hang-ups was the Old Testament. It's full of the good, the bad, and the ugly—sex, murder, genocide, natural disasters, a bunch of lists, and detailed building descriptions. But how do these things relate to my faith in Jesus?

Without going into too much detail (as there are many other books that focus on this topic alone), I hope to present a basic framework of some of the bigger storylines in the Old Testament. When read as a narrative, as is the form of so much of the Old Testament, it's evident that the individual stories are woven into the fabric of the overall narrative. As storytelling communicators, it's of paramount importance that we identify and articulate the Master Story. In regard to the Old Testament, theologian N. T. Wright describes it as "couched not in the terms of later philosophy but in the narrative of God and the world, and particularly the *story* of God and Israel" (*Evil and the Justice of God*, 45, emphasis added).

Early in Genesis we see that God created a good, beautiful creation with great care and attention to detail. God makes it very clear that this is his intimate handiwork, and his creation of human beings is the culmination of this handiwork. It's a perfect world made with perfect intention. Then things get out of order. In chapter 3 we see the rebellion in the garden of

Eden when humans disobey God's one command not to eat the fruit from the tree of the knowledge of good and evil. In chapter 4 we see the first murder, which leads to widespread violence in chapter 5.

Finally, we observe in chapter 11 how the people come up with the crazy idea of building a tower—what we now call the Tower of Babel—that's supposed to reach up to the heavens. What's the human race—which God created in perfection—doing with what God's given to us? In response God scatters the people all over the earth and confuses their languages so they can no longer pursue their "great" ideas.

But God doesn't give up on humanity; instead, he finds someone willing to start putting it back together the way God intended it. In Genesis 12:1–3, we find God speaking to Abram (later called Abraham):

> Go from your country, your people and your father's household to the land I will show you. "I will make you into a great nation, and I will bless you; I will make your name great, and you will be a blessing. I will bless those who bless you, and whoever curses you I will curse; and all peoples on earth will be blessed through you."

So God has charged Abraham to bring renewal to a people who've turned from the way of God. He promises that God will bless this nation (Israel) and that, ultimately, it will bless others by pointing them back to the one, true God. It's evident that through Abraham and his family, God will bless the whole world.

Now at this point, the story takes turn after turn as God's chosen people, Israel, are on a quest to bring the world back to the way it was originally intended. Many of its leaders are brought up to power, and many leaders fail. In fact numerous times the biggest hurdles in the mission of Israel were the Israelites themselves (Exodus 15:22–24; 32:1).

As we continue the story of Israel that started with Abraham and was carried on by Isaac and Jacob, we find that after the death of Joseph, the Israelites are reduced to slavery. But God hasn't forgotten his promise of renewal, restoration, and the mission of bringing the world back to its originally intended form.

In Exodus 3:14–17, God talked to Moses: "I AM WHO I AM." He said further,

> This is what you are to say to the Israelites, "I AM has sent me to you." God also said to Moses, "Say to the Israelites, 'The Lord, the God of your fathers—the God of Abraham, the God of Isaac and the God of Jacob—has sent me to you.' 'This is

my name forever, the name you shall call me from generation to generation . . . I have promised to bring you up out of your misery in Egypt into the land . . . flowing with milk and honey.'"

God is known to the Israelites as *Yahweh* or their God (monotheism in a polytheistic world), which creates more intimacy between God and his people, as well as more connection between God's Story and the characters he freely chooses to tell it. Yahweh's promise to Moses came true: God led the Israelites out of their slavery in Egypt, and they began their adventure to the Promised Land. That's the story of Passover, which is still celebrated today. Of course, we know the story isn't over. Later on, the people ask God for a king. First, they get Saul; but they're eventually led by the "man after [God's] own heart"—King David (1 Samuel 13:14).

The story of the people whom God chose "to bless the world" (by putting things back together) continues in a saga that leads us to a book of stories compiled by an educated Jew. The book is Daniel, and it "emphasizes the underlying hope that the whole world will somehow be brought to order under the kingship of the one creator God, YHWH, the God of Abraham." (*Simply Christian*, 79) Of course, this doesn't happen quickly enough. However, Daniel also prophesied that a Savior would be central to the story and finally bring the mission of Israel to a climax, returning the world to the way God had originally intended. We know that man to be Jesus.

This is the bigger story—the story I'd missed for so long. It's full of interesting characters, plot twists, and changing settings that we all can be part of and do our best to share with the world around us. The Old Testament story doesn't end with Jesus' arrival; it continues. And it's in his life, death, and resurrection that we find the climax to the Christian story and to where I turn for much of the proceeding. I turn not only to the story that Jesus embodies but to the stories that he tells.

## The Story Continues

The story continues with us—today. Jesus came to complete the task—once and for all—of putting the world back the way it was originally created to be. Jesus teaches us to pray, "Your kingdom come, your will be done, on earth as it is in heaven" (Matthew 6:10). As such Jesus wants to continue this restoration and renewal process with each one of us. Jesus wants all of us to take part in the story that started way back when he first called on Abraham to be a blessing to the world. Therefore, when our lives become centered in the way of Jesus, we take on a part of this mission of putting things back together.

This renewed understanding of the Bible and its core message has great implications for us as Christ-followers. We now can see that we're not merely bystanders waiting for the world to pass us by so we can apathetically waltz into heaven and roll around on golden streets. We aren't inhabitants of the Earth so we can destroy as much of our natural resources as possible because, "It's all gonna burn anyway!"

N. T. Wright notes further: "The Bible is there to enable God's people to be equipped to do God's work in God's world, not to give them an excuse to sit back smugly, knowing they possess all God's truth." (*Simply Christian*, 184) Indeed we're called to be active participants in God's mission to bring the world back to the way God intended. The story continues . . . and we are some of the main characters.

> "The Old Testament isn't written in order simply to 'tell us about God' in the abstract. It isn't designed primarily to provide information, to satisfy the inquiring mind. It's written to tell the *story* of what God has done, is doing and will do . . ."
> *Evil and the Justice of God*, 45 (emphasis added)

I believe this generation is poised to make a huge impact in this chapter of God's story as told through humanity. Many teachers of this generation are taking this mission seriously and doing their best to live that out in an effort to bring positive change and be examples to our youth.

## Expanding the Dinner Table

A teenage "couple" within the community of youth I serve has taken the mission of Jesus seriously. Most high school couples spend most of their time whispering on the phone to each other (while their friends and family do their best to listen closely), or they begin planning their wedding vows because they've found their "one and only." (I hope you don't sense my teenage relational cynicism!) But this particular couple has chosen to use their combined energies to do good within our community. They're doing their best to join God's mission of putting things back together.

Over the last three years (and they continue today), they've served at a local women's shelter in an extremely forgotten part of a nearby town—an area most parents wouldn't allow their kids to enter. (Actually, I'm still not sure how they pulled that one off. Sorry if I'm blowing your cover, guys!)

Every Monday night they and a couple of their friends prepare dinner and then sit down and share conversation with about twenty women who'd otherwise receive very little attention. Most every time I talk to these young volunteers—before I can even say "Hello"—they share a cool story or tell me about a new person they met during their Monday night dinner. It's obvious they're serving Jesus in that place. "For I was hungry and you gave me something to eat, I was thirsty and you gave me something to drink, I was a stranger and you invited me in, I needed clothes and you clothed me, I was sick and you looked after me, I was in prison and you came to visit me . . . The King will reply, 'I tell you the truth, whatever you did for one of the least of these brothers of mine, you did for me'" (Matthew 25:35, 36, 40).

For a good part of their first year of service at the shelter, they asked my wife and me to serve with them. Monday is my day off, so I always found a way to excuse myself from going with them. But then Christmas rolled around, and they decided to throw a Christmas party for these women with whom they'd built relationships. Once again, they asked my wife and me to come out and celebrate with them and the women. I can't remember exactly how it happened (my wife probably talked some sense into me), but we decided to attend the party.

It was magical. These women lit up with such surprise and honor when they walked into the room and saw there were people who cared enough to do something like this for them. The women were open to my wife and me, but they were *connected* to these teenage volunteers. There was immediate conversation, storytelling, and laughter between them. At one point in the evening, I pretended to wash dishes so I could hide out and simply take in the whole scene. I hadn't cried since my wedding day (and all my wife could do was laugh at my altar breakdown). But for me, this scene was so right, so pure, so much of what God intended for his people that I couldn't help but shed tears.

## Little Josh Radle

This kid somehow snuck into our middle school ministry when he was in sixth grade (we only have seventh and eighth graders) and began wreaking havoc. One evening we played [chicken volleyball. (Two teams circle around their own bed sheets on opposite sides of a parking lot and take turns launching a raw chicken at the other team.] Josh decided his team was moving too slowly with the sheet, and it was time to take things into his own hands. So this 4' 11", eighty-five-pound kid ran as fast as he could to the chicken's predicted landing spot. Everyone stared up at the chicken and then down at Josh in pure disgust and anticipation. When the chicken came down, Josh caught it just below his chin—and it slid down into his hands. A circus catch for the ages.

That's Josh Radle.

While Josh is often the kid who drives me to premature graying, he's also the one you want around most because he's willing to experience anything. Three years pass, and we begin to wade through a heavy story that involves a homeless man named Henry and two very self-consumed teenage boys. Every day the two teenage boys rode their bikes to the shopping center to play video games and buy candy. They'd ride right by a homeless gentleman, and every day they hurled degrading comments and random items at him. Later, one of the boys experienced a death in his family that made him think about the way he'd been living. In the end, the boys saw Henry as someone they could serve and love in the way of Jesus. It's a story designed to articulate and invite these teenagers into participation in the Kingdom of God.

A few weeks after we completed this story, our teenagers threw a large Thanksgiving dinner that our community sponsored for the local marginalized, lonely, and poor of our small, rural town. It was the kind of party Jesus told his followers to throw (Luke 14:13). With loads of leftovers the day after the meal, I asked Josh if he wanted to go with me to give away our extra food to some people who needed it more than we did. Josh and I spent the rest of the day meeting with great people who were not only starved for food, but also to be cared for. We drove to a number of locations around town and hung out with these people. And each time we got back in my truck, I could see that Josh's eyes had been opened a little bit more to what could be done if we used our energy for serving "the least of these" as Jesus articulates through his parable in Matthew 25:40. At the start of our drive to pass out the food that day, he was pretty quiet as he soaked it all in. (This kind of behavior was rare for Josh, so I was concerned that he was sick or something.) But by the end of the day, he was telling me about other places where he'd seen people who needed food, and he insisted that we go to these places. So we did!

But the truly amazing part is that one of the last places we stopped on the way back to the church campus was a spot behind a Mexican restaurant where Josh said he and his buddies used to ride their bikes past a homeless guy—just like the story we'd been going through. We drove to the restaurant, grabbed some Thanksgiving dinner, and walked up a trail where Josh

TEACHING THROUGH THE ART OF STORYTELLING

remembered seeing a homeless guy. Sure enough, there was a gentleman lying on his old, beat-up mattress and drinking warm beer under a tree.

For the next thirty minutes or so, Josh and I got to hear this man's story, and we began developing a relationship with him. In fact, we later learned (after telling this story at one of our adult gatherings) that the man's sister is part of our church community. And the whole congregation has since rallied behind this gentleman to show him the love of Jesus by caring for his everyday needs.

Little Josh Radle has chosen to become part of the story. He's come to the realization in a very tangible way that God's redemption story is still being played out through his people. Josh understands the bigger story that's still being told today, and he's chosen to become an active participant within it. Josh has seen the face of Jesus through the "least of these" and is on a mission to partner with God in putting the world back to the way God originally intended (Matthew 25:40).

> I have talked about the fact that God is working in history to bring about this new age. There is the danger, therefore, that after hearing all of this you will go away with the impression that we can go home, sit down, and do nothing, waiting for the coming of the inevitable. You will somehow feel that this new age will roll in on the wheels of inevitability, so there is nothing to do but wait on it. If you get that impression you are the victims of an illusion wrapped in superficiality. We must speed up the coming of the inevitable.

> —Dr. Martin Luther King, Jr.
> *Facing the Challenge of a New Age (1957)*

We must make our way into the story.

# 2

# FOLLOWING JESUS' EXAMPLE

Jesus was the ultimate communicator.

He spoke to the people of his day on many levels. He called out the religious elite, lifted up the insecure and needy, offered hope to those who couldn't find any, and he did it all with a profound understanding of his culture and its history.

While Jesus was a master storyteller, at other times he needed but a few words to make a point that could be felt in the very fabric of a listener's being.

Jesus was a literary genius. In his sermons and parables, he frequently used foreshadowing, irony, and word parallels that either clearly made his point or left the listener wanting more.

Jesus had a very powerful message, and he wasn't afraid to communicate it. At times he engaged what many Christians today might call secular culture, as seen in his embracing of the Samaritan woman at the well (John 4:8–10). The Samaritan culture was despised by the religious of the day, yet Jesus was willing to go out of his way to cross through their villages (Luke 9:51–56). Further, Jesus wasn't afraid to offend the close-minded (Jesus' defense of adulterous woman against religious elite—John 8:7–8) or challenge spiritual rebels (Jesus' response to money changers—Matthew 21:12–13).

Jesus was the ultimate preacher, speaker, and storyteller; and we must grow into a better understanding of the kind of communicator Jesus was. Because he saw himself as one who helped others discover the truth for themselves, Socrates called himself a midwife. He focused on asking more questions than offering answers in the hope that learners would come to their own insights and observations. "Jesus is very 'midwifey' through his

25

use of questions, stories, and parables." (Alan Hirsch, *The Forgotten Ways*, 166) While we should seek to bolster our self-confidence in regard to communication, the first priority should be to rely on ourselves less and on Jesus more. We'll be disciples who study, listen, learn, and follow our Rabbi closely.

In this chapter we'll take an extended look at one of the primary ways Jesus communicated (storytelling) and explore how we can learn from his example. More than a third of Jesus' teachings were carried out through the art of storytelling—and most often they were fictional stories he created based on his understanding of the culture, his audience, and the topic he was working to convey.

But before we get too far into the conversation of Jesus' storytelling, it's important that we first take a look at and understand the setting into which Jesus was born.

## A Jewish Story[1]

"The message of Jesus must be understood in the context of the first century. Jesus was Jewish. He spoke Hebrew. He lived and worked in the land of Israel when his people, the Jews, suffered under the cruel yoke of the mighty Roman Empire. He lived his entire life as a religious Jew . . . The story of Jesus' birth in the Gospels resonates with Jewish beliefs concerning God's plan of salvation and the promised coming of the messianic deliverer." (*Jesus the Jewish Theologian*, 197 and 3)

At the time of Jesus' birth, there were distinct divisions between ethnic groups, religious beliefs, and political systems. It was a world of opposition. Your ancestry decided whether you were this or that. Your beliefs were tied to this god or those gods. You were under this political system or that political system. Most importantly, much of the *this* or *that* in which you took part had almost nothing to do with your *decision* to be a part of this or that, but with where you were born and what family you were born into. And the reality was that all three of these paradigms (ethnicity, religion, politics) were connected.

For example, if you were born into a Jewish family in Jerusalem, you would immediately be under the reign of the warring ideology of the Roman Empire—and you didn't get to choose any of these realities. They were

---

1. Thanks to Brad Young for his research and commentary on early Jewish culture and theology, specifically in regard to this parable.

inherited. You simply embraced the culture, beliefs, and political systems that you were a part of from birth.

Into this complex and conflict-filled scene, a boy named Jesus is born. True to the form of past prophets and significant characters in the story of Israel (Isaac, Jacob, Moses, Isaiah, David, and John the Baptist), Jesus' arrival as king of the Kingdom fulfilled prophecy and offered renewed hope to an exiled people (Isaiah; John 1:26, 27). Jews of the day understood this was no coincidence. In fact, right off the bat we see the Jewish Scriptures coming to life when the angels sang a song of praise to the Messiah. The prophecies have come true!

> Glory to God in the highest, and on earth peace, good will toward men.
>
> (Luke 2:14 KJV)

This Messiah is here to bring peace and restoration to the conflict! This is big news for the Jews of the day.

> In light of the descriptions of supernatural happenings associated with important figures in Jewish history, the angels' appearance and their hymn of praise are very much a part of the fabric of Hebrew thought for the messianic idea. The anticipation that the birth of the Messiah would be heralded by the angels of the divine presence was by no means foreign to popular thinking in the first century.
>
> (*Jesus the Jewish Theologian*)

Immediately Jesus' mother and father must get creative in order to avoid his death at the hands of the Jewish government. (Of course we know how the religious leaders in Jerusalem responded to Jesus' claims as Messiah!)

Jesus was dealt a very specific hand of cards: He was born into a Jewish family and lived in a small town under Roman rule—not forgetting that there was just a little influence from the dealer.

Jesus began his journey to maturity within the Jewish culture. Significantly his culture provided an educational system created to bring up God-honoring Jews to carry on the name and traditions of the religion. There were many inherited expectations and obligations that a young Jewish boy would have to fulfill as he grew up in this culture. From the ripe age of around six, he'd start his study of the Torah, or Pentateuch, the first five books of the Hebrew Scriptures. Jewish boys typically learned from their local synagogue's rabbi.

Over the next decade or so, these boys' studies expanded from the Torah to the whole of the Hebrew Scriptures, and their lives revolved around their study and application of the Hebrew Scriptures (in other words, the Christian Old Testament). They lived and breathed this text and were taught to fall in love with it just as God loved them so much that he offered them these pure and sacred Scriptures. Within this text Jewish boys would learn and memorize all of the stories that filled its pages. They would study the characters and try to make sense of how they all fit together. In fact, in this culture most everyone had all of these stories memorized because there were so few scrolls of Scripture. Most often there was only one scroll per village, therefore the words, the teachings, and the stories became central to all who learned in this Jewish system.

The rabbi was the local youth pastor, of sorts. He taught these youth in the same ways that he learned while growing up and added the new things he picked up along the way. Many rabbis taught aspiring disciples using not only the stories of the Hebrew Scripture, but also fictional stories they'd created to illustrate a point. These story illustrations were called Jewish *agada*. In rabbinical theology, teaching through Jewish *agada* helped create a mental picture of God's grace, mercy, and unlimited love.

Each rabbi embraced a specific way of describing doctrine (i.e., the primary way he interpreted the sacred Scriptures). The rabbi's goal was to identify which students—who hoped to be disciples someday—had what it took to carry on the doctrine of the rabbi. In other words the question was: *Who could understand, embrace, and pass on this interpretation of the Hebrew Scriptures to the youth of the future?* So the rabbi's reputation was placed in his students' hands. For this reason very few students who studied under the rabbi were accepted as disciples. Most didn't make the cut and were sent back to their families to learn trades from their fathers. (For a more detailed look at the relationship between a rabbi and what were called his *talmidim*—students or disciples—check out followtherabbi.com.)

In regard to Jesus, we know he was called "Rabbi" when he started his formal ministry at the age of thirty (John 1:38). Knowing that the twelve-year-old Jesus listened to and answered the questions of the rabbis in Jerusalem, it's very likely that this educational system wouldn't have been foreign to him (Luke 2:41–51). Naturally, a student's understanding of the Scriptures and his ability to communicate it were greatly influenced by his rabbi's teachings. No wonder Jesus did so much of his teaching as a rabbi through the art of storytelling—or as we more commonly say . . . parables. So Jesus understood the stories of the Old Testament, he learned through Jewish *agada*, and now he was to become one of the most effective storytellers in history.

If Jesus learned of the power of story and believed in it enough to use it as a teacher, then shouldn't we follow our Rabbi's example?

## The Messiah's Superpowers

As we studied in the first chapter, it's of paramount importance that we understand Jesus' birth and life as part of the larger story being told throughout Scripture. After all, his life was the culmination of so many storylines. Many kings ruled over Israel before Jesus came on the scene. At their best they acted as appointed mediators between God and humanity; at their worst they severed the connection between God and humanity. Jesus was the newly inaugurated king of the Kingdom, but his rule wouldn't resemble those of earthly kings. He wouldn't restore humanity through the conquest and overthrow of Caesar, nor would he glorify Jerusalem or the Torah to the extent of past kings (Matthew 5:21–28). Instead Jesus' coronation would be on the back of a donkey; he wouldn't sit upon a golden throne—but instead hang upon a wooden cross. All would be invited into this Kingdom, and those who formerly were last would now be first (Matthew 20:16). While Jesus' presence was anxiously awaited, the form of his reign was quite a surprise for those expecting a traditional king to conquer and build. He was God's ultimate example of the redeeming restoration intended for the earth. Jesus brought the kingdom to earth and offered us a way to finally put things back together . . . to make things right.

This was the story the rabbis of Jesus' day knew so well. They waited for the coming of the Messiah who would be empowered by Yahweh, who not only acted earlier in the Story but would once again act on their behalf today. Jesus received this Spirit, this divine power, to accomplish the mission of redemption.

> "God's salvation is the kingdom of God, and it means that—at last—God has acted to deliver humanity and now reigns over all of life, and is present to and with us, and will be in the future."
> Stassen and Gushee, *Kingdom Ethics*, 29

Rooted in the Jewish belief that God is good, the messianic idea develops from a sense of past history and future destiny. Just as God saved his people in the past, he will deliver them again. In the past he used an anointed prophet like Moses. In the future he will use a chosen servant empowered by the Holy Spirit. The glory of the divine presence (Shekhinah) is revealed in the work of the future prophet who will be anointed to accomplish the task.

(*Jesus the Jewish Theologian*, 21)

Before Jesus starts his missionary work, John baptizes him in the Jordan River. Something transpires here that's central to our understanding of the power of Jesus and the prophecies that were coming true. As we read in the third chapter of the Gospel of Luke, Jesus is baptized with others, affirming the redemptive role of John the Baptist, while at the same time revealing his own identification with humanity. After Jesus comes out of the water, we read that the Holy Spirit descended in the form of a dove and a voice from heaven affirmed Jesus' role as the supernatural Son of God (Matthew 3:16). It's as though Jesus is given the stamp of approval to carry out his mission from the very God who's worked in such powerful ways for so many years as recorded in the Hebrew Scriptures.

This brings us back to the rabbis' understanding of the Messiah who was to bring redemption under the leadership of the Spirit of God. After Jesus' baptism a divine presence settled on and dwelt in him; it was known as *Shekhinah* (pronounced shuh-KHEE-nuh)—and God's glory came to rest and hover over all that Jesus said and did. This *Shekhinah* was to be brought to the world as a reminder that God's glory, his presence, is everywhere—the whole world is saturated in it. Jesus was the divine representation and example of *Shekhinah*.

There's one more important rabbinical note essential to our discussion regarding how Jesus learned and the life he calls others to live. Salvation, or becoming of a follower of The Way, was far more than receiving forgiveness of sins and anticipating heaven after you die. Jesus calls people to a more comprehensive idea of salvation—one that not only assures eternal salvation, but also sees the eternal as starting . . . now. It requires Jesus' followers to begin the process of restoration in the here and now. The rabbis of Jesus' day called this reality of living in harmony with God *Olam Haba*, translated "World to Come."

In the same way, repentance is an act of not simply confessing sin, but of turning from one life to a brand-new life centered in the ways of Jesus. (To get a better understanding, it may be worth researching the Hebrew word *T'Shuvah*.) Jesus, a rabbi, called his followers to *Olam Haba*—a life marked not only by salvation, not only by repentance, but also by continually moving toward closer harmony with God. (Rob Bell, *Velvet Elvis*, 16)

So after his baptism and supernatural affirmation, Jesus sets off on his mission to bring about a new way of seeing and experiencing *Shekhinah*. It's interesting to note how Jesus begins his ministry: He doesn't summit a mountain and start spouting his Old Testament knowledge or revelations about this new way of experiencing God. Rather, he hangs out with the people. Then he finds some average guys working in their fathers' trades—meaning they'd dropped out of "rabbi training"—and Jesus asks them to be his disciples! Finally, he spends an extended amount of time just hanging out with and healing the sick and hurting. Word of this revolutionary rabbi, Jesus, spread across the land (Matthew 4:24). He was turning much of the inherited conflicts, stereotypes, and religious legalism on its head and replacing it all with good news—news that called for a new way of life covered by the *Shekhinah* of God.

## Homegrown

Jesus understood the importance of establishing credibility with the people to whom he was about to offer the most radical, countercultural messages in history (the Sermon on the Mount). Jesus didn't assume that others would accept what he had to say without first understanding who he was. In contrast, how often do we assume credibility from our listeners? Do we take the time to earn the right to say what we have to say?

That said, Jesus understood his audience. He wasn't an interloper. He grew up in this culture. He was a part of the religion, had family and friends in the area, and was active in the trade of carpentry. His reputation was already in place. If he had something to say, there was very little reason why people wouldn't be drawn to listen to him.

This reminds me of my first Sunday in my current youth pastor position. Just thinking about it makes me cringe, laugh, and almost want to cry, all at the same time. I was a product of a much different ecclesial model from where I'd worked for two years—a big church consisting primarily of middle-to-upper-class members with a program steeped in "excellence." Sunday morning youth ministry as I knew it involved standing in front of the kids while they sat in neat rows of padded folding chairs and offered me their undivided attention. (No, I'm not lying!)

I went to the adult church service a few times before I was hired, but I hadn't been to the youth gatherings. So today was my big day to win hearts and intellectually stimulate the minds of teenagers in a way they'd never experienced before! I "knew" youth ministry—now it was time for everyone to step aside and let the master take over.

Of course, to be an effective communicator, you have to use PowerPoint. But the youth room at the time didn't have a projector or TV! And for some odd reason, the chairs in the room weren't lined up correctly! So without hesitation, I decided to move the class to a room containing padded chairs and a projector screen. This was the perfect place to mold young minds and launch the youth ministry's new beginning like a blue herring over the mighty Mississippi.

I stood at the front of the classroom with my notes neatly prepared and a cool screensaver projected on the wall, and I watched the kids file in. To my surprise, their faces were covered with looks of confusion, disorientation, and, well, disgust. My tidy youth ministry bubble was being blown open like a window in a hurricane. Things were not looking good for the new guy.

Not knowing of any other options at this point, I decided to press on. Throughout my teaching, a number of youth equal to the number present at the beginning of class wandered in as though they were watching the good old days evaporate with each word from my mouth. Still, I offered the lesson with dazzling eloquence and stunning PowerPoint illustrations! But no one cared. In fact, the only thing they cared about was exactly when things would go back to normal.

It was clear I didn't understand my audience. I was walking into a death trap, and I didn't even see it coming. It wasn't that I was trained incorrectly. I'd entered into a different context with different people and different ways of doing things. I didn't know that PowerPoint was as foreign to them as a razor is to a man with a lifelong beard. Or that sitting in neat rows of chairs and listening to one guy speak for thirty minutes was something they knew only from their painful experiences at school. Or that half the group never showed up on time because there were either really good waves that morning, or they had to walk to church because their parents didn't want to support that "religious stuff."

Understanding and relating to our audience with some form of credibility is paramount to our ability to communicate effectively. Jesus knew this and was willing to continually read his audiences over the three years in which he actively communicated. There were times when he spoke to religious Jews, and others when he spoke to pagans (namely the Hellenistic culture). There were times when he spoke to the rich, and others when he spoke to the poor. There were times when he spoke to the politically power-ful, and others when he spoke to the politically oppressed.

We don't have to read very far into the Gospels to know that Jesus spent a lot of his time speaking to and challenging the religious elite regarding the way they taught the faith. He often called them *hypocrites*, a word that described stage actors in that day. Once again, Jesus used his culture to make a point, challenging these leaders to do better than stand on street corners and disfigure their faces like actors to show how "holy" they were (Matthew 6:5, 16).

## Parables

It's important to remember that Jesus' parables sometimes contain hidden messages. And the messages aren't always clear. Numerous times in the Gospels, Jesus tells a story and doesn't explain it, leaving the disciples to scratch their heads. Sometimes the messages are packed deep in cultural understanding, and other times they play out through characters and scenes that could be viewed from many different angles. Yet Jesus left a lot of room for conversation and interpretation.

### The Parable as Puzzle

My Hebrew professor at Fuller Theological Seminary once told my class that he'd heard parable defined as a "puzzle," which he originally sourced from his language professor. I was intrigued by this understanding.

As we know, a puzzle consists of many different pieces that come together to make one whole and comprehensive picture. Without all the pieces there's at best a fractured semblance of the intended image—since each piece is unique, necessary, and often beautiful in its own right.

When you get only a fleeting glimpse of a piece of fine art, it's impossible to fully appreciate its beauty; if you take time to study its complexities, however, you attain deeper levels of understanding. The same is true for the parable as a puzzle. The parable story gradually offers small glances at a work in progress that's building on itself. With each piece that drops in place, the story exposes formerly hidden truths. What's interesting is that the pieces of the parable puzzle may not create the same image for each listener, who assembles them in unique ways specific to his or her life experience and worldview.

In the same way, our artfully created stories may affect one teenager in a completely different way than another. Therefore, the most important variable is that the story *is* meeting them in some way, whether it inspires some listeners to give away all they own to the poor or develop a better relationship with a close friend. Only remember that as with a puzzle, our created stories have pieces, too—characters, plot, and setting—and listeners may relate to one "piece" more than another.

Let's take a closer look at how Jesus used Jewish *agada* through the parable of the prodigal son to convey a powerful message to his audience. We'll cover a basic summary and then discuss Jesus' strategic use of setting, characters, and plot within this story.

## Breaking Down the Parable of the Prodigal Son

In Luke 15:11–32, Jesus uses a parable to describe the relationship between a father and his two rebellious sons. Typically the main focus of this story is geared toward the younger son—hence the traditional name of "prodigal son." But research surrounding the original context in which Jesus told the parable makes it overwhelmingly clear that this is a story about *both* sons' rebellion—each man was equally guilty of disrespecting the role of the father. On the same note, it's also a story primarily focused around the loving and gracious father who allows his sons free will but hopes they'll eventually accept his unconditional love.

The parable describes the younger son requesting his early inheritance and then wastefully spending it all in a faraway country. Meanwhile, the older brother stays home and continues to work for his father. The younger brother runs out of money and can't get help from anyone, so he turns his sights back to his father's home. Not to the liking of the older brother, the father welcomes his younger son home and insists on throwing a party for his son who "was lost and is found" (Luke 15:24). Throughout the story, the father is in the role of a helpless parent who compassionately stands behind his sons regardless of the decisions they make.

## Setting

Jesus' use of setting within this story was determined by the context of the traditional family of the day. So many of the key elements (for example, inheritance, family dynamics, location, the very spiritual act of returning, and so on) were central to the culture of Jesus' day.

Let's first look at how the original audience would understand the illustration of inheritance. When the younger son asks for his inheritance before the father's death, he's making a very bold request. In essence he's asking for his father to die. What did the father think when his son made such an audacious request? This point would have sent the original audience into a state of shock and dismay.

The people also knew that, as it's recorded in the *Mishnah*, Jewish law allowed the father to divide his estate before his death. Therefore, the audience would understand that the inheritance was *divided* between the brothers, with the older brother receiving two-thirds and the younger brother one (Luke 15:12). In addition, the Mishnah makes it clear that the sons aren't allowed to let anyone take possession of the land until the father is dead (Baba Bathra 8:7). The sons can sell the land, but they're actually selling the rights to the land once their father has died. For this reason, the potential price they can get for their share of the inheritance will be greatly under the market rate because the buyer has to wait an undetermined amount of time before taking over the land. Again, when the audience hears that the younger son sold his inheritance, they'd understand the ramifications of an early sale, which adds greater meaning to the story.

That said, the father still has rights to run the estate and give orders to the servants even after he's handed over the inheritance. All of these dynamics and intricacies are assumed in the story Jesus created. He understood his setting and spoke directly to it.

Now let's take a brief look at the family dynamics of the day and compare them to the setting Jesus creates in this parable. In this culture the older brother has the great responsibility to act as the mediator and voice of reason within his family. The "eldest brother" was expected to lead his siblings by example and be aware of any interfamily conflict or undercurrents that might result in conflict. In this parable, however, the older brother stays silent while the younger brother seeks his premature inheritance from their father. Big brother goes with the flow of events, takes his share of the inheritance, and stands by as a witness to this broken relationship between the father and younger son. Again, this response would have told Jesus' audience a lot about the character of the older brother. They would have perceived him as being as much of a rebel as the younger brother—just in a different form. To Jesus' audience this would be a story about the prodigal *sons*, rather than the prodigal *son*.

Next, let's consider the significance of the parable's location. All the elements of the story tell us that the father's estate is part of a Jewish region.

Thus, when the younger brother sets off for a faraway country, we understand that he's no longer dealing with fellow Jews but non-Jewish foreigners. When the money runs out, one of these strangers is benevolent enough to offer him a job, but the younger son still can't get food in this distant land. This is a significant point, and it leads to the final element of the setting.

As previously stated, the act of repentance (or returning to your first love) was very symbolic and significant to the Jewish audience of Jesus' day. At this point in history, the Israelites understood themselves as being central to God's redemption and healing process for all mankind. As recorded in the Old Testament, there's a long history of exile and restoration throughout Israel's past—the act of going away and coming back . . . or returning. And at the time Jesus tells this story, Israel had made its way back to its original land but was still feeling the effects of its most recent exile. They were uncomfortable in their own shoes, so a story about someone returning to a loving and compassionate father was a beautiful and reassuring message.

## Characters

### Main Character: The Father

Some may disagree with my interpretation of who's the main character in the story, saying the younger son fills that role. But I view the father as being the lead in this example of Jewish agada. Like so many movies, books, and stories today, the father is the Christlike figure in this parable—a symbol of all that's good. He's full of grace and compassion and loves his sons so much that he doesn't manipulate their free will to make their own choices. At the same time, it's obvious that he's hoping each of his sons will make choices that benefit not only the individuals, but also the family as a whole. The irony is that neither brother fully understands the father's love. Both men misinterpret how to "gain" his love, and the father simply waits for them to figure it out.

### Supporting Character #1: The Older Brother

While he isn't the poster boy for "Big Brother 101," he is—

- A hard worker
- Faithful (although, as we later find out, with the wrong intentions)
- The brother who receives the larger inheritance
- Wise with his inheritance (not selling when the market was bad)

- Jealous and easy to anger

A few things he isn't—

- Slow to judge (see Luke 15:30)

- A mediator

- A loving brother and son

- An older son who understands and embraces his inherited role within the family

It's clear through Jesus' telling of this parable that the older brother doesn't understand the loving relationship between father and son. He views his father only as an employer who's there to offer him his earned wages and a grand reward—his inheritance—when all is complete. He believes he can simply work his way into a right relationship with the father—that it must be earned. Much like the highly religious person who's missed Jesus' central message of grace, this character performs actions only in an attempt to earn a love that already exists.

We can see that the older brother is gravely wrong in his understanding. The father loves him all along and is just waiting for his oldest son to embrace that love and experience the beauty of their relationship. The older brother finds it easier to judge others instead of honestly evaluating himself, which leads to hostility rather than brotherhood. In addition, he allows jealousy and anger to form a wedge between his brother and himself. Again, he misses out on the beauty of relationship. He's unwilling to give or receive forgiveness, which keeps him from experiencing the profound and spiritual act of *return*.

### Supporting Character #2: The Younger Brother

Of course his role is essential to Jesus' point; but as we've seen, it's not the only storyline Jesus hopes we take away from this parable. The younger brother wastes his inheritance. He takes his father's money and runs as far as he possibly can from the person who loves him most. He creates a barrier of distance between the endless love of his father and himself. (How many of us also run away from our Father thinking we can escape his view and endless love?)

The younger brother runs until he hits rock bottom. At this point he's faced with a decision: Does he continue to run and do his best to make things work through his own efforts? Or does he begin the profound process of repentance by turning a 180 and seeking reconciliation with his father? (Again, I recommend reviewing the Jewish *Teshuva* process.)

Like his older brother, the younger son misinterprets his relationship with his father. Like his older brother, he also views his father as an employer when he hopes to be offered a job as a servant in his father's estate. But the father once again reflects the traits of God our Father through his willingness not only to forgive his son, but also to celebrate his return. "He was lost and is [now] found" (Luke 15:24).

## Plot—The Primary Message the Story Is Designed to Convey

A creative and detailed plot is central to an effective story. In this one Jesus creates a plot with four scenes:

- Scene #1: Jesus offers an explanation of the characters and the division of the inheritance (vv. 11–12).

- Scene #2: Younger son sells inheritance and wastes money in a far-off country (vv. 13–16).

- Scene #3: Younger son repents and father celebrates (vv. 17–24).

- Scene #4: Older brother is angry and father explains his love (vv. 25–32).

Each scene builds upon the prior one. They not only make sense to the ear, but they make sense to Jesus' audience. There is drama, a stage, and rich content to each character that make this an exciting and engaging plot with storylines weaved into it. In the first scene, we see a free offering from the father when his younger son asks for his inheritance. This is followed by the younger son's rebellion and distance, while legalism and apathy are evident on the part of the older son. Next, we're drawn to a turn in the story that leads to repentance and reconciliation with the younger son. And finally, regarding the character of the older brother, we're left hanging at the end of the story. He's unwilling to embrace the love of his father, and he won't accept or forgive his younger brother.

Jesus leaves the outcome open to the audience's interpretation. It's as if he's presenting a story that could be true in any of our lives, and now it's time for us to come up with the application. How is the story going to end? Jesus won't give all the answers; instead, he compels us to look in the mirror and ask ourselves the hard questions: *Am I going to accept the Father's challenge to love and be loved? Am I willing to forgive my brother in the same way that God has forgiven me?*

Jesus, the Master Storyteller, uses this ingenious story to convey a message of unconditional love, the importance of reconciliation between family members, and the role of individual repentance, which can be seen through Israel's opportunity to return home through Christ's redemptive work to a God who never left them.

## Finally

By taking this detailed walk through Jesus' example of the art of storytelling, I hope we can see more clearly how we can create stories that impact others today. In later chapters we'll discuss and learn how to create stories with settings that take into account the contexts of our audiences, develop characters through whom we can tell stories, and formulate plots that communicate powerful messages.

I don't know if Jesus sat down and carefully prepared these stories to be so culturally profound or if he simply used his supernatural gifts as a communicator on the fly. But in either case, he gives us a sterling example of storytelling that communicates a profound message while understanding the culture of the audience. If we as communicators and storytellers—after the study of this book and our own personal reflections—can tell stories with half the cultural understanding, theological application, and heartfelt love for people that Jesus had, we'll be in pretty good shape.

# PHILOSOPHY
# OF TEACHING
# THROUGH STORY

# 3

# THE SCIENCE OF LISTENING: MORE LINEAR AND FLOWING THAN STRUCTURED TEACHING

Although I've spent one semester as a seventh and eighth grade science teacher, I definitely don't claim to be a scientist. In fact I don't even claim to know much about science in general. Growing up I was the kid who got good grades in just about every subject . . . except science. In the early years, when a good grade constituted a pretty crayon drawing of the solar system, I could keep my grades up. But when we moved into atoms, lipids, and charts that make the quadratic formula look simple, my "BS" (as we called it) couldn't hold up in the grade book.

At this point I realized that science wasn't my calling. But instead of trying to tough it out through the hard classes—like a "good" student—I simply found a loophole in the system. For example, when it was time for me to plunge into the wonderful world of chemistry, I knew it was time to start doing some research. And it wasn't chemistry research, mind you, but "how to avoid taking that class but still graduate from high school" research. Well, if there was one thing I knew how to research, it was cutting corners in my education. (How else do you suppose I managed to graduate as salutatorian?) These weren't illegal or unethical corners; they were simply corners that many (who weren't lazy enough?) didn't discover because they failed to research them.

So before my senior year began, I found out that an astronomy class offered at a local junior college would count as my third year of science in place of chemistry or physics. On top of that, half of the class sessions were taught in the planetarium where it was pitch-black and there were comfortable seats, allowing for a quality nap. I got an A in that class—the last science class I ever took.

Now that I've "successfully" lost all credibility in the field of science, I'd like to discuss the science of listening. However, I'd like to add that since my days of science avoidance, I've been intrigued by it, actually studied it, and have encountered some amazing stuff.

## Neurologically Friendly

Teaching through the art of storytelling creates a medium for the listening mind to activate in a linear, flowing manner. Before I go on, I must offer that every brain is created and works differently. As such, I'll speak to general trends and information on the brain and its workings in relation to learning. (Also, I'll refer to the brain as the "mind," as it's more appropriate for our conversation.)

Listening is central to the growth and development of most human beings. Studies show that 85 percent of what we know we've learned through listening (Shorpe). Yet we only remember 20 percent of what we hear and 75 percent of the time we're distracted, preoccupied, or forgetful (Hunsaker). So, we understand that listening is really important, but it can be a highly inefficient way to transfer information depending on the mode of communication. Some argue that offering convincing statistics engages the listener and creates lasting impact, but studies also tell us that people quickly dismiss statistics that are inconsistent with their beliefs (Graesser).

But fictional stories—which can be processed very efficiently with minimal effort and high recall—offer "suspension of disbelief," which can lead to tangible change (Bower & Graesser). For this reason, some in the medical field have implemented storytelling as a mode of healthcare communication, bringing attention to issues such as suicide and AIDS prevention.

So we're left with story—the telling of which can break down walls of cynicism and mental distraction and lead listeners toward engagement. The art is in assimilating fiction into belief, which is why intentional dialog and discussion is pivotal to its success.

## *Pura Vida!*

As I compose these words, I'm sitting at the kitchen counter of a small, rustic cottage on the beach in Costa Rica, home of some of the best waves in the world. My church was gracious and caring enough to give my wife and me a three-month sabbatical for renewal, restoration, a time to write, and the chance to visit family and friends across the globe. It's been great so far, other than the fact that I'm still working very hard to figure out how to actually *slow down*!

The pace of my life at home shouldn't be viewed with respect but (mostly) disgust. I *say* I do my best to keep limits on my activities, but I don't believe I really do. This choice has negatively affected many I'm closest to, so I sit here in Costa Rica while trying to kick some nasty habits.

If you've been to Costa Rica, then you're probably very familiar with the term *pura vida* ("pure life"). This is the mentality and spirit of most everyone who lives here. For example, they typically start work at 10 a.m. But if the surf's good that morning—no problem, starting at 2 p.m. is just fine, too. A busy day can be defined as walking to the local supermarket and checking your email on the dial-up connection, or trading an afternoon of chores for a healthy conversation. (There's even a Web site dedicated to the idea: www.puravida.com.)

On the other hand, if you aren't accustomed to it, *pura vida* can be very frustrating. In fact last night my wife and I were driving all over the place on a quad that we'd rented for the day. It was the only day during our month in Costa Rica that we splurged and had transportation that wasn't powered by our own legs. So on this day, I was hoping to get as many things done as possible while we had a "quick" form of transportation at our disposal.

This wasn't a good remedy for my disease of busyness that I'm working so hard to overcome. As soon as I sat on the throne of this symbol of efficiency and speed, I was a man on a mission. I had about ten things "we" needed to get done before the seven hours of rental time ran out. Fortunately, my wife is much healthier than I am in this area, and she simply looked at me like I was a crazy man and felt free to say so as well.

One of my planned stops was at the local surf shop. A week or so before, I'd bought a board there because I was desperate to catch a few waves. But it ended up being an unwise purchase. The board was terrible, and I'm sure the shop workers were making fun of me the moment I walked out the door. Anyway, this was my day to sell back the board (at a fraction of the price for which I bought it) so I could get a different substandard board that suited me a little better.

We needed to return the quad to the rental shop by 6 p.m. But at 5:35 p.m., I was still standing in front of the surf shop, waiting for the store to reopen. Every day the shop closes for the afternoon so the owner can surf, but it's supposed to reopen at 5 p.m. So I waited and waited . . . and waited. Meanwhile, my wife stayed as far away from me as possible because she could see my frustration building and the sweat pouring down my face.

FINALLY, the owner showed up with wet hair and a surfboard under his arm. "Sorry I'm late, but the waves were just too good to leave today." I thought, *I could have been surfing those good waves if you'd gotten back here in time!* But the more we talked, the more I realized he was a great guy, and I could learn a lot from him. *SLOW DOWN, Jon. Don't expect everybody to cater to you and your needs,* I thought. And when I pulled in late to return the quad, the owner didn't mind at all because it was all about *pura vida*! I'm starting to learn.

The reason I tell this story is because I believe we can get ourselves into this toxic, fast-paced mentality when it comes to our teaching habits, and it directly impacts our teenagers' ability to engage in the bigger biblical story we discussed in the first chapter. It's easy to adopt the mentality of "If they don't hear *everything* now, then they'll never hear it again." I can understand that way of thinking, and I'm sure it comes from positive convictions. But I'd like to offer some history into where and why we may have taken on this anti-*pura vida* mindset in our teaching.

## Constantine and Christianity

Way back in the 300s, there was a fierce military warrior by the name of Constantine. He was on a mission to take out the powerful military of the Roman Empire, led by Maxentius. As you can imagine, defeating the military of an empire meant you'd then take over the empire and become the new emperor. For Constantine there was a lot on the line here. Who wouldn't want to sit on a golden throne and be served grapes and wine all day long?

Well, on the night before his big battle with Maxentius, Constantine was taken by a vision that communicated to him that he was to paint the "heavenly sign" of the cross on his soldiers' shields. He did just that, and the next day he and his soldiers (with their cross-bearing shields) won a battle just outside of Rome. With the victory came the capital and the complete reign of the Western Roman Empire. Constantine was now in control.

As we know, an empire has a huge impact on the culture of its land, including its spiritual belief systems. The vision of the cross and the subsequent military victory was all Constantine needed to legalize Christianity as not only the accepted, but also the privileged religion of the Roman Empire in the Edict of Milan of 313. Before this declaration was made, Christians were persecuted and usually not accepted. They were termed *superstitio,* "denoting an intolerable deviation from society's norms of behavior." (Alan Kreider, *The Change of Conversion and the Origin of Christendom*) Such a shift to the top of the heap could only be a good thing for the future of authentic Christianity, right?

Leading up to Constantine's reign, the process of conversion to Christianity was a very slow one that required great commitment as demonstrated not only through word but through deed. An authentic conversion was identified by one's heart of service and love toward the church and all people. To become a Christian involved far more than an overnight, one-time decision. It required a commitment that led to a distinct lifestyle change. It was deliberately and painstakingly fostered by mentors, teachers, clergy, and family members. Follow-up and guidance were greatly valued. In his vision for authentic discipleship Neil Cole says, "We want to lower the bar of how church is done and raise the bar of what it means to be a disciple." (Cole, *Organic Church: Growing Faith Where Life Happens*, 50)

In addition, the way of the Christian required a disavowal of violence and killing. It also meant that Constantine would need to get off his throne from time to time and care for the poor and visit the sick. In other words, he'd have to reassess his whole lifestyle. But at this point in his personal life and political career, Constantine wasn't willing to change. Yet he still liked identifying himself as a Christian. The more Constantine studied and evaluated the cost of being an authentic Christian, the more he decided to make things cater to his own lifestyle and political system.

Let me be clear: There are many times I don't get out of *my* chair— which is definitely not a throne—to help the poor and visit the sick. But this new way of viewing the life of a Christian as one who "said" more than he "did" had huge implications for future generations of believers.

It wasn't until Constantine was on what was apparently his deathbed in 337 AD that he finally submitted to the life of an authentic Christ-follower, not just the "idea" of it. But even this event brought disillusionment to the people of the Roman Empire. It soon became common practice for people to wait until they were on their deathbeds to "fully commit" themselves to Christianity just so they could escape the high calling of the lifestyle of a Christian. This was called "clinical baptism," and it was common up until the point that infant baptism became the norm. (*The Change of Conversion and the Origin of Christendom*)

This is when the perception of Christianity really got blurred. As the fourth century progressed, Constantine and his successors offered attractive incentives for one's conversion to Christianity, including preferential treatment from church leadership, immunity from public duties, job perks for civil servants, and an overall respect for aligning with the emperor's religion. As a direct result, church attendance and membership shot through the roof, and anybody and everybody was now a "Christian."

The following is a part of an insightful conversation that my friend Mark Scandrette once had with a gentleman, and he told Mark: "'Jesus is cool, it's just that they have f–ed with Jesus. I mean, Christianity was at its best when it was secret and hidden and you could die for it.' This profound, if crass, statement recognizes that the power of the gospel lay in its ability to be a countercultural and revolutionary force—not just a story to believe, but a distinctive way of life. The man's comment prompted me to consider these questions:

- Am I in some measure complicit in the domestication of Jesus?

- Has my desire to maintain social status or a standard of living forced me to disregard the revolutionary nature of the life and teachings of the master? (*Soul Graffiti*, 32)

- What happened to the development of a relationship with Jesus and the practical application of his ways?

- Where was the mentoring, teaching, and pastoring that was so essential to authentic growth in the life of a Jesus follower?

- Is this truly what Jesus intended his followers to believe and act out?

Things got worse in the Roman Empire for those who didn't align with the Christian religious institution. Those regarded as pagans had a hard time finding jobs, only "Christians" could join the military or civil services, and infant baptism became mandatory. Augustine commented, "For long, Christians did not dare answer a pagan; now, thank God, it is a crime to remain a pagan." (*Enarrations in Psalm 88*) It seemed Christians had things under control; God's power—which was what pre-Constantinian Christians claimed was the center of their cause—was now less important. Critical thought and individuality were not the norm in this era's cultural, political, and social climate.

## Aftershocks

As a direct result of these historical events, the teaching of the religious Christians took a turn in a whole new direction. In response to the "clinical baptism" that had become so common starting with Constantine, preachers and theologians developed a new genre of sermon that contained threat and appeal. Much had to do with "not delaying" their salvation and was communicated through solemn monologue and increased theatrics. In reference to the "awesome" and "hair-raising" writers of the day, it was said, "A powerful emotional and psychological impression [was put] upon the candidates in the hope of bringing about their conversion." (*The Search for the Origins of Christian Worship*, 219)

Does this sound familiar? Do we intentionally or unintentionally "speed up" the conversion process in our listeners, whether out of love or arrogance? If so, what kind of faith are we calling our listeners to? An institutionalized, socially acceptable norm? Or are we allowing Jesus' story to captivate and take hold of each individual's heart? Our coercive teaching strategies won't bring about authentic change; the power of the Holy Spirit does that, unlocking the desire to participate in the revolutionary story of Jesus that's still unfolding today.

I believe many of us teachers and communicators are prime candidates to fall victim to this arrogance within our teaching. For those of us who've taught for extended periods, it may be easy to assume we can just put it on cruise control. We believe we can fall back into the lap of teaching that was once considered effective and expect our beautiful deliveries filled with humor, irony, and drama to clearly communicate the message of Jesus. Or we may believe that since we've been with these teenagers for such a long time, we know what they need—it's simply our role as communicators to feed them their needed spiritual meals.

> "Far too long, historians have accepted the claim that the conversion of the Emperor Constantine (ca. 285–337) caused the triumph of Christianity. To the contrary, he destroyed its most attractive and dynamic aspects, turning a high-intensity, grassroots movement into an arrogant institution controlled by an elite who often managed to be both brutal and lax."
> Rodney Stark, *For the Glory of God* (Princeton University Press, 2003), 33

Or how about those of us who just graduated from college or seminary and believe we're arguably the best communicators or theologians since

Billy Graham? It all seemed so clear in school, and we got lots of As. So now it's time for the easy work of harvesting souls, right? Everyone will be blown away by our superior knowledge and charisma and—BOOM! The masses may now come forward.

Gregory of Nazianzus, who was in Asia Minor during the era of Constantine, once offered himself as "the director of your soul." We must take our roles as pastors, shepherds, teachers, and communicators seriously, but we must never take ourselves too seriously. It's not that we can't be confident; it's that we can't be arrogant. Only then can we be fully dependent on the Spirit. May our teaching never take the form of calling our teenagers to an "immediate" conversion out of our arrogance based on a personal misinterpretation of who we are and how we view our roles.

Further, I believe this "speed it up" mentality in our teaching can be a direct result of our inability to trust in a God who's sovereign—over every situation and every heart. Again, we begin to take ourselves too seriously. We avoid story because such a method of communication often prevents us from experiencing the satisfaction of spiritedly "pounding home" our profound points. But so what? Sometimes that intentional focus on a point may be necessary, but it's often more powerful and pointed when attained through conversation. Don't get me wrong—this art of storytelling stuff can be hard on our modern, Western mindsets. Slow. Deliberate. Time consuming. Patience-trying. It takes humility and willingness to evaluate our own motives and habits as teachers. I hope we'll always leave far more room for the Spirit's direction than for our own.

As we studied earlier in this chapter, the science behind teaching through story tells us that we're engaging the mind in a healthy and thought-provoking way. So . . . how about getting a little *pura vida* in our teaching and try slowing down enough to allow that to happen?

## Less Preaching, More Conversation

Teaching through the art of storytelling is designed to provoke more questions than answers. It's primarily a conversation starter, not a conversation finisher. This isn't always true, of course. As youth listen and engage in the story, they can process some of the answers because the story meets every teenager in a different spot of their faith experience. The story can stand alone if it's well prepared, conceived, and directed. That said, in general I don't see the stand-alone story as being the most effective.

Where the story is the conversation starter, the follow-up discussion and dialogue is the conversation continuer. (I would say "finisher," but most often that's not the case.) It's paramount that we communicators open up times of honest dialogue and questioning. Just like a rousing conversation after a good movie, most of the impact and application will occur after we tell the story. It's like spending a large amount of time setting the table and displaying a beautiful meal, and now it's time to call our guests to sit around the table and take it all in. We communicators become not simply the primary medium for communication but hosts of a feast of questions and conversation. The meal is set; now it's time to enjoy and discuss its preparation process, its nutrients, and the effects it can have on each one of us. It's a beautiful thing.

> "Jesus was also aware of his audience—told parables that raised provocative questions and invited people into the process of exploring the answers."
> Dick Staub, *Culturally Savvy Christian*, 169

Does this mean we simply offer up our opinions and spiritual insights through our stories and then let them all be cast out into a sea of subjectivity? Absolutely not. It's very important that we keep the group centered on the topic while still leaving room for honest conversation and questions. (I offer some insights and discuss the tangible applications of this process in more detail in chapters 6 and 8.)

However, we must keep in mind that our teenagers are *told* things all the time, whether they're at school, on the sports field, at home, or in some form of relationship. Let's allow our preaching to give way to guided, thoughtful, and Spirit-led conversation in the hopes of inspiring them to begin the process of entering into a living, active, and very real relationship with Jesus.

## If Only I Had a Guitar in My Hands

I have a friend named Taylor. He's been a part of our high school community for the last three years or so. For the most part, he attends our gatherings and is well liked and respected by his peers, as well as the "older folks" who hang around (also known as "the youth staff").

Taylor is a guitar freak. He plays it, listens to others play it, and flat-out *lives* it. And I have no doubt that he'd be proud of that description. He has the long curly locks of most "good" rockers, a penchant for tie-dyed shirts, and an endless supply of Converse shoes. When I ask Taylor what his favorite activity is at any given point in the day, he puts his index finger over his closed mouth and ponders his response. Fitting to his character, he responds, "I would have to say either listening to guitar riffs of my favorite artists on CD or playing my guitar without distraction." This kid would *eat* his guitar if such a feat wouldn't scratch it.

Taylor also is a very intellectual and thoughtful student of the Christian life. He's not afraid to ask hard questions, and he's a model to many regarding how to live a life of honest transparency and openness to accountability. I respect him very much. That said, Taylor has a hard time focusing during any kind of teaching because he self-admittedly drifts off into guitar world within about two minutes of the start of the talk. He recently told me (during a time when I was *not* teaching through story, incidentally) that he was really interested in what I had to say and would like to know more. But he just couldn't pull himself away from pondering how to "play that A-minor with a harmonic that the Allman Brothers nail every time" in one of his favorite two hundred songs of theirs. (I felt so affirmed and self-assured in regard to my teaching abilities after hearing that—defeated by an A-minor with a harmonic. Awesome!)

As a result while Taylor would often come to our weekly gatherings on Thursday nights, during the talk he'd either play his guitar (outside) or do his best to listen for at least a few minutes. Then we started a new story. I don't remember the topic exactly, but there was something about it that caught Taylor's attention. And not the two-minute span I was used to seeing, but twenty minutes of attention followed by thirty minutes of dialogue attention. At this point I began wrestling with some of the ideas in this chapter. Scientifically, what was it about storytelling that allowed an otherwise hard-to-capture mind like Taylor's to actively participate in what I was saying? There had to be something to it. And apparently there is.

# 4

# BEING PART OF THE STORY ENGAGES US—WE CAN IDENTIFY WITH AND RELATE TO THE CHARACTERS

When I was growing up, my dad loved to tell stories to my sisters and me. He'd tell stories about the stupid things he did in his childhood, or the times when he and his family would go on some great adventure. Occasionally he'd even make up a story that somehow—through his divine "dad powers"—we actually believed and couldn't get enough of.

My favorites were the ones when he read our favorite books to us. There was something about the way he read them, and the way I was able to picture the whole scene in my head. I wouldn't look at him, but I'd stare at the ceiling and go into my own story world. I could picture myself as a part of it. There were times when I even believed it was my story. And then my dad would throw in his own little twist that led to the happy-go-lucky main character getting eaten by a shark in his swimming pool or falling into hot lava. My sisters and I rarely surmised right away that it was dad's creation. But then it would click, and we'd get shaken out of our daydreams and start dog-piling him.

Some would consider this example merely a reflection of childhood, but I believe we all can relate to stories in this way to some degree. There's something about stories that engage not only the mind, but also the heart. We become part of the story. We picture ourselves living out this life that's being revealed to us, and subconsciously we relate it to our own.

As we continue to discuss the philosophy (or why) we should teach through story, I'd argue that we should teach in this way because the art of storytelling engages listeners to the extent that they can relate to and become part of the story.

## Back to Jesus' Example

When we're teaching or communicating, our goal is to pass on messages to our listeners. If we create an atmosphere that draws in our teenagers to the point where they're actually engaging with or becoming a part of the topic we're presenting, then I'd say we're doing a pretty good job. Stories— or Jewish *agada*, as we discussed in the third chapter—allow us to get to this place where our listeners are transformed from mere bystanders in the conversation to active participants.

"The main Jewish traditions have to do with the *story* of the creator and the cosmos, of the covenant god and his people . . . It should therefore be clear that the parables, by their very form, place Jesus firmly within his Jewish context."

N. T. Wright, *Jesus and the Victory of God*, 176

Again, let's look at the example of Jesus and the parables he so eloquently delivered during his three years of intentional ministry and teaching. "In the world of Jewish *agada* (storytelling to illustrate a message), Jesus creates striking word pictures so that everyone can understand what God is like." (*Jesus the Jewish Theologian*, 130) Jesus didn't create stories involving palaces, thrones, and gold when he was talking to the common people of his day. No, he created stories that revolved around the context and real-life situations of the people he was speaking to. Jesus did this because he wanted to engage his listeners. Jesus wanted his message to go from being a list of doctrines or principles to becoming a story that each individual could relate to and take part in. The Jewish *agada* so effective in Jesus' day are still effective today, more than two thousand years later.

One of the most influential speakers and communicators of the twentieth century was Dr. Martin Luther King, Jr. He was born in Atlanta, Georgia, into a middle-class, African-American minister's family. For the majority of King's childhood, teens, and early twenties, he was surrounded by a middle-class, often white, culture and setting. He went to private schools and graduated from college with a sociology degree, which allowed him to enter a primarily white seminary in Pennsylvania. After graduating he went on to receive a Ph.D. in systematic theology from Boston University.

Believe it or not, King didn't experience segregation and hate to the same extent that most southern African Americans did. It wasn't until he moved to Montgomery, Alabama, that he finally tasted so much of the pain of oppression and segregation that southern blacks had been experiencing for so long. So how did this man, with his relatively affluent and privileged upbringing, engage and transform the perspective of oppressed black people in the South?

King became a speaker who engaged not only the minds, but also the hearts of his listeners. He understood his audience, and he began speaking their language. His ability to engage listeners brought on one of the most powerful revolutions in the history of the United States.[2]

If, in pressing for justice and equality in Montgomery, we discover that those who reject equality are prepared to use violence, we must not despair, retreat, or fear. Before they make this crucial decision, they must remember: whatever they do, we will not use violence in return. We hope we can act in the struggle in such a way that they will see the error of their approach and will come to respect us. Then we can all live together in peace and equality.

(Martin Luther King, Jr., *Our Struggle*, 1956)

## The Good and the Bad

There are a few things we should discuss before moving forward. First, communicating through story doesn't work all of the time for all of the people. From what I've seen, there's a certain level of humility and a willingness that listeners must demonstrate in order to engage in and be a part of the stories we tell. It takes humility in the sense that listeners must trust your ability to tell a believable story, while humbly opening themselves enough to apply it to their own lives. This is no easy thing. We all know kids who simply don't want to hear anything we have to say.

In addition, listeners must be willing to entertain our stories as effective tools for contemplation, conversation, and, ultimately, for life change. Just like any form of teaching, the effectiveness is going to come down to how the listener chooses to receive and act upon what's being presented. It's ask-

---

2. Pages xiii–xxi of introduction written by James M. Washington in *I Have a Dream: Writings and Speeches that Changed the World.*

ing a lot for the hearer to participate with both humility and willingness—neither one is easy to come by. In large part, however, I believe these are areas we must leave up to the Holy Spirit to prompt and lead. (Although, I'll add that I've found storytelling to be an easier medium for communicating with that "difficult" listener than most other forms I've experimented with.)

Second, we don't want to create a fantasyland in which listeners become so consumed that they can't fathom a way to relate it to their own stories. If we're to engage our listeners, then we must do so in a way that leads them toward positive change, not confusion. We must be careful how we use this powerful tool and move forward as shepherds who are looking out for the best interests of each of our listeners.

## It's Not Just a Bunch of Theories

I can remember working on a story that I was planning to share with a group of high schoolers. Its main focus was depression, loneliness, and the destructive act of cutting. (In case you're not familiar with cutting, it's a form of self-injury that's gained much popularity among individuals looking for a physical release of their emotional pain.) The story's main character, Chloe, had a serious case of "spiritual bulimia" after growing up in a Christian home that became a bubble she felt she had to stay within.

Chloe put on a show for her church community and family so no one would suspect she had any issues. And she was never encouraged to be the real, raw, dynamic person she was created to be. This brought her down a destructive path that developed into a deep depression and fear of authenticity. And it ended with the act of cutting as a medium of release

**What Is Spiritual Bulimia?**

"I did my devotions, read all the new Christian books and saw the Christian movies, and then vomited information up to friends, small groups, and pastors. But it had never had the chance to digest. I had gorged myself on all the products of the Christian industrial complex but was spiritually starving to death. I was marked by an overconsumptive but malnourished spirituality, suffocated by Christianity but thirsty for God."

Shane Claiborne, *Irresistible Revolution*

from her pain and confusion. (See chapter 10 for a full version of the story.)

As I told this story to these high schoolers, I realized it was hitting home with one particular teen. It was obvious that she was humbly and willingly engaging in this story, probably because it was one she could relate to on many levels. She was one of the most fun and outgoing girls in our community. It was a rare occasion when she wasn't the center of attention and leading a group of teenagers into some ridiculous act or conversation. She was a very lovable and seemingly genuine person. But as Chloe's story unfolded, I could see the tension and pain creep into this teenager's face. In fact a couple of weeks into the telling of the story, I noticed she couldn't listen to it anymore. So she left the room and drove all the way home.

I wasn't sure what was going on. But after I didn't see her the next week, I assumed there were some major issues. Her small group leader had also noticed her absence and her recent odd behaviors. So I asked this leader to track her down and see how she was doing.

About a week later, the small group leader finally got in touch with this girl. She said she wasn't able to get the whole story yet, but the girl felt as though the story we were telling was *her* story, and she couldn't bear to deal with the emotions it was bringing up. We learned that she'd also been living a life full of fake smiles that were simply masking myriad issues. She'd been taken by spiritual bulimia at a young age, which led her to simply spew out the "Christian" answer to every question so everyone believed she was the perfect flannel-graph Christian. She'd built up so many walls that the people who thought they knew her best couldn't see her true person. She was surrounded by people but completely alone. This led to depression and eventually to cutting.

This youth chose to be engaged by this story. This ancient form of storytelling—Jewish *agada*—had become so real to her that she could wrestle with some of the biggest issues she'd ever faced in her young life. She heard Chloe's story and realized that it was *her* story, too. She didn't want to deal with it, but she knew there was no other option.

To some, this art of storytelling may sound childish or elementary, but through Jesus' example and other examples we see today, we know it engages not only the mind, but also the heart. We're engaging precious hearts, souls, and minds. May we be encouraged by this opportunity to partner with God in changing the lives of those who need it most. And may we be very aware and sensitive to lead only in a way that uses this medium for personal engagement and in a way that God sees fit.

# 5

# USING OUR STORY-SATURATED CULTURE

Standing in an ocean of people I'd never seen before, I felt a connection. This was the place where each of our personal stories connected and became one story, if only for a few glorious hours. Most of us stood on the floor looking up at Mason Jennings, a poet-activist-folk musician . . . and our favorite storyteller. Based on the responses of those around me, it seemed that each of us felt like he was telling our story. Of course, many of us were interested in different things, and some of us had *very* different moral and spiritual convictions. But for now, in this place, we were able to put that aside to be a part of something bigger.

This was not a "Christian" concert or rally but rather a kind of conversation. Yet in this place, there was a sense of oneness. The lyrical sharing of lives and the stories that made up each of them was very real. And I could sense God here. God may not have been thrilled with what many in the crowd were doing (based on some of the aromas I smelled from time to time), but that didn't keep God from showing up in a real way.

Standing with my wife and a group of friends, I was blown away while listening to our voices singing songs in unison that asked profound, raw questions and called for change in the here and now. These songs looked at the parallel between the characteristics of Jesus and Dr. Martin Luther King, Jr. We were engaging in a message communicated through a beautiful, rhythmic medium that prompted many voices to rise together:

*Dr. King, I think often of you and the love that you learned from Jesus.*

*Alabama, Alabama . . . Bethlehem.*

*Dr. King, I think often of you and the love that you learned*
*from Jesus.*

*Up ahead we have a mighty task, love the face behind hatred's*
*mask, on the day we understand our past, God Almighty*
*we'll be free at last.*

*Alabama, Alabama . . . Bethlehem.*

I wonder to this day—did everyone really wrestle with what they were singing? "Love the face behind hatred's mask." A call to move past helplessness and violent response toward a third way of treating others who harm us. To my ears, it sounded as though these words in our sing-a-long were at the cores of our hearts and visions for a better world.

Mason continued by telling his story of disenchantment with religion and the church. He spoke of wanting more, of truly wrestling with the characters of God and Jesus:

*Jesus are you real, did I make you up? Is salvation what you*
*want or is faith enough? . . . Are you just a word I use when*
*I don't understand?*

*Jesus are you stronger than a loaded gun?*

*All I do is doubt you God, all I do is love you God, all I do is*
*question you . . . what else can I do? All I do is search for*
*you . . . what else can I do?*

*And when I mean I search for you, I mean I search for peace. I*
*search for hope, I search for love and one day for relief.*

*I'm not a man of faith, I'm a man of truth. But this feeling in*
*my heart, is this feeling proof?*

*Are we left in the dark or are we left here in the light? Seems to*
*me that both are true and it's up to us to know what's right.*

*God give me strength to accept the things that I just cannot
know, even when I lose control I will not let you go.*

Again, as I heard the masses sing this together, I was overcome by the power of the moment. These were questions so many of us were wresting with. I could hear the tone of the crowd grow in their passion as they sang out these questions about Jesus, faith, politics, and salvation—a disconnect between dreams and realities that drew those in attendance to the significance of these questions. Unlike so many other songs that deal with relationships and random experiences, there was something about these words that engaged people.

One part of me wanted to scream out the "answers" that had been fed to me for so many years while growing up in my cozy Christian bubble. But that wasn't the language this group was speaking. That wasn't the language they needed to hear. They needed a place to voice frustration, to ask questions, and to seek change together. And because of this common connection created through a story being told so eloquently and artfully, I felt as though I could sit down for coffee with any of these folks and have generative conversation on a wide variety of topics.

## Where Does the Power Come From?

Why is there so much power in a shared life story? Why is there so much passion, frustration, and energy pent up in so many of us that we need a place like this venue to let it all out? Have we as Christians offered a place for these frustrations to be vented and questions to be asked? Are we calling others to engage in the powerful story of Jesus and offering ourselves as examples of what that may look like?

There is something powerful about a shared story. The story may be one of hope or despair, pain or relief, failure or success, questions or answers, hate or love, loneliness or friendship, brokenness or redemption. Our culture is saturated in endless storylines, and some of the most influential people are telling them. Instead of running from these storylines, how can we be active participants within them, doing our best to bring about positive change that leads back to the ultimate story of Jesus?

## A Call Away from Our "Christian" Alternatives

I believe one of the biggest reasons there's such disconnect between Christians and non-Christians (even when they share similar stories) is because of all the labels we've created—especially those of us who call ourselves Christians. I believe these labels start with the very terms *Christian* and *non-Christian*. It's almost as though we're creating terms that allow us, as imperfect human beings, to decide who's "in" and who's "out." And the labels spiral endlessly into a pool—no, an ocean—of "palatable" alternatives that we Christians sign off on as acceptable, pure, theologically sound, or God-honoring. The sad part is that most of these labels are used on T-shirts, bumper stickers, and pins, as well as in movies, and, most frequently, in music. "If it's 'Christian,' then it's okay," says the wary (or is it weary?) parent. That might be one of the greatest deceptions within the Christian subculture—naming what's "good" and what isn't, what meets the criteria and what doesn't, what God approves of and what God despises.

This paradigm has greatly demoted the beautiful and lively **noun** of *Christian*—one who answers a living, breathing, challenging call to follow Christ—to an **adjective** that is sometimes used to promote slimy, deceptive marketing traps for the unseeing.

I believe that Christians best embody Jesus' radical to discipleship when their lives reflect a social alternative in a similar way that Jesus' life rejected the trappings of empire. That said, the Christian subculture has in some ways traded this radical call for the production of cheap "alternative" products. It seems that Christians have made alternatives for most everything in our culture—movies, music, T-shirts, bumper stickers, books, and so on. This creation has wandered from what may have begun as a well-intentioned vision to what's now become a multibillion-dollar industry. I believe Christians already do plenty to isolate themselves from the real issues and culture of the day. So maybe we're most needed right in the center of our culture, where we can create change from the inside.

I'm not advocating much of what exists within our culture, or even saying this role is appropriate for everyone. But I do believe there are many beautiful and godly things that happen within it. I believe it would take a lot more faith to engage culture with a heartfelt vision for positive change than to create our own safe bubble within it. Oftentimes the good intentions behind "alternatives" can be seen, but I propose we get a little more creative and do our best to move forward in a posture of illuminating the good that already exists.

God isn't confined to things that use the confusing, often misleading adjective *Christian*. In fact there are *many* resources that fall under the label *Christian* that would be absolutely toxic for my teenagers to take part in. I'm typically more wary of the resources *with* that label because it's as though they've been given a free pass to present an issue or topic without proper accountability and critical evaluation. For years I've been asking my teenagers why we use the word *Christian* as an adjective. Was it ever intended to be used in that way? Let's ensure that it remains in its true form—as a beautiful noun!

Every year there is a "Christian" music festival in my area that presents many samples of thoughtless attempts at art and says they're honoring to God. But to me, it seems there's more of a focus on making money from tasteless and even offensive "Christian" merchandise than on honoring and teaching a life lived in the Way of Jesus. Now, I know from firsthand experience that some great things have transpired as a result of this event. Things that I'm sure have affected the lives of many in a positive way. But I have to ask the questions:

- Is this really the best way to represent the God we're calling people to serve?

- Is this gathering of Christians what we want others to use to define Christians?

- Are the monetary and personal gains justified to "put on" a show . . . for ourselves?

For all of these reasons, my heart broke one Thursday night when a teen walked into our weekly gathering wearing a T-shirt emblazoned with I'M THE CHRISTIAN THAT SATAN WARNED YOU ABOUT. I immediately assumed where he'd purchased it, but I asked him anyway, as that was about the only positive thing I could come up with at the time. He told me he purchased it at this particular event. Then his brother walked in with a "Christian" alternative to a common T-shirt of the time: RELIGION IS EVERYTHING, THE REST IS JUST GUITAR.

What kind of faith does that represent to our culture? What kind of life are we calling fellow Christians to live? One that represents the same greed and offensive attributes that "we" get angry about in the "non-Christian" culture? Or one that's creatively trailblazing different ways to live that call Christians to bring about positive change and offer hope to a world that needs it? The part that saddened me the most about these T-shirts and the precious kids who wore them was the realization that this Christian "industry" had finally gotten to . . . us. This "Christian" marketing and moneymaking empire had successfully brainwashed the innocent and undeserving into thinking this was the way Christians should live and be portrayed. They did it. No wonder there's such disconnect between the common stories of Christians and non-Christians!

But with this heartbreak came a resolve to contend for the faith—with a renewed passion for calling others to truly wrestle with and live out the characteristics of love, peace, hope, wholeness, faith, compassion, and partnership. To call others to truly *be* Christians. We can't let this "us versus them" mentality derail opportunities to hear others' stories—even when they represent differing values or beliefs—and share our own stories.

I believe this "us versus them" mentality shows up strongest in the relationship between the West and the Middle East. My wife and I had the opportunity to study in Israel last summer, and we spent a significant amount of time in the West Bank/Palestine. We met a Christian Palestinian couple who live just outside Bethlehem and run a non-profit organization that promotes peace and reconciliation through the arts. One morning we crossed through the haunting checkpoints between Israel and Palestine and spent time with kids whose lives—while suffering a terribly oppressive situation—had been given a glimmer of hope as a result of this revolutionary couple's work. As we sang (in Arabic!) and danced with these kids, we experienced the Kingdom of God raining down upon the earth. This couple's native language is Arabic, they are Arab Palestinians, and they love Jesus with all their hearts. From a Western perspective our friends might have been labeled "terrorists" before we ever had the chance to hear their story. Thankfully Jesus' Story transcends all political, social, and cultural barriers.

As we discussed in chapter 2, Jesus was born into a world with much religious and political conflict. Jesus came to elevate the conversation beyond religious posturing and political gain toward the advancement of the Kingdom of God. He came to offer a third way. It was no longer about "us versus them"—it was simply about him (Ephesians 2:12–19). Jesus' message was such a radical statement of peace that it was offered to both Jews *and* Gentiles. This was a huge statement based on their conflicting history! Are we people who experience, share, and live out Jesus' story (message) with believers and nonbelievers? In order to appreciate the beautiful symphony of God's kingdom, we have to hear all of the instruments.

Now, one of the primary roles we have as teachers and communicators is to encourage our youth to see the connection between the stories that exist within our culture. We must encourage them to break down the walls of stereotype, prejudice, and differing opinions and find common storylines within our own personal stories and the stories of those we seek to engage. And all the while we must be examples of these unifying traits: Lives that don't give in to the polarity of our Christian, political, or socioeconomic subcultures.

## Our Story-Saturated Culture

Those of us who choose to teach through the art of storytelling have a lot going for us based on the primary modes of communication our culture uses. Most people, but especially teenagers, are consciously or subconsciously captivated by some form of story. It may be a movie, poem, book, short story, or song; but each communicates a story, and our culture is often very receptive to each of these forms of storytelling. There is rarely a Friday or Saturday night that the local movie theater isn't packed with people of all ages looking to be told a story through a powerful medium. Some hope for relief from their difficult situations, even for a short time; others hope to learn about and partner in a newly presented cause; and still others simply want to be entertained.

Hopefully, based on the points that were developed in the previous two chapters, we can now see why some of us shed tears at various points during well-crafted movies. Or how about the times when a movie ends, the credits roll, and everyone stands up and claps at a large piece of white screen hanging from the ceiling? Such is the power of story.

Something about pre-feature trailers forces me not to miss them. My wife knows this very well. There are times when we're running late to see a movie, and I know we'll miss the previews, and I'm tempted to turn right around and call it a night. For me, there's something larger than life about the anticipation I feel when the screen goes black before and after each trailer leading up to the main feature. We anxiously wait to jump in head-first and take part in a newfound adventure, sense the birth pangs (or death throes) of a beautiful relationship, or just laugh at some ridiculous circumstances. Why is it that every time we watch *Braveheart*, we shed tears and are overwhelmed by an urge to wear kilts and moon someone? (Or is it just me?) Anyway, our minds are drawn to story, both scientifically in the brain and emotionally in the heart. We engage.

How about little kids? From the day they're born, they're surrounded by various superheroes, with their own special powers that they use to save the world. By the time kids turn three, they're wearing superhero pajamas and pretending to fly off the living room stairs with blanket corners stuffed inside the backs of their shirts.

Why is it that older teens in our youth ministries often remember only the stories we tell and not the points we were trying to convey through those stories? One of the main reasons I first considered the idea of teaching through story was because of this revelation. How in the world can these kids still remember a story I shared three years ago about me jumping from a tree, missing the trampoline, and breaking both of my feet, but they haven't got a clue as to the point I was trying to get across with that teaching? Once again, the story offers lasting and impacting communication.

One of my dad's favorite pastimes is sitting with a glass of orange juice on the back porch on a Saturday morning, soaking in the early sunlight, and listening to Garrison Keillor on the radio. I remember waking up to the sound of Keillor's voice many a Saturday morning while growing up. Keillor is an artist—a master storyteller who creates fictional stories around fictional characters in a fictional town. His stories about the town, Lake Wobegon, are filled with humor, irony, and bathed in the context of the Midwest. In contrast, my dad is a very driven man who takes great pride in being an active father, employee, and husband. Most every Saturday is filled with projects on the house or some activity with the family. But when it comes to Keillor's *Lake Wobegone Days*, there is always time to slow down and get lost in this sacred art of storytelling.

We can see that story captivates all ages, from the superhero-pajama-wearing three-year-old, to the teenager who remembers only the embarrassing stories we share, to the father, employee, and husband who stops his busy life long enough to hear just a little more of the story unfold. We're all drawn to it. We're even drawn into it. That brings me to my next point.

Story is very versatile. It can be used to inspire us to action. It can motivate us to look at the world a little bit differently. It can force us to reflect on the past, whether good or bad. It can make us forget some of reality as we're brought to laughter. It can be used to make a point that needs voicing. It can engage our hearts to partner in something bigger than ourselves.

You may have noticed that many organizations that exist to champion—or seek resolution for—a specific cause don't seek partnerships with others through a three-point outline. They do it through story. We hear about the fourteen-year-old girl who's given an opportunity not only to live another day, but also receive an education and a future as a result of this organization's efforts. Or we learn about the mother, wife, and friend who received medical treatment for her cancer because of generous gifts and donations. Or we see the photos of kids standing in front of a new school that was built in their low-income area as a result of a few people who took an interest in their stories. There is power in story. We're inspired by the good and stirred to action by the bad.

Our culture is filled with stories. And the youth with whom we're communicating are part of that culture. They understand the way we communicate when we use the medium of story, and doing so places us one step ahead of the game—there's one less degree of separation. Now we can put more energy into application.

This is why we teach through the art of storytelling. Teenagers have heard the story, and we can now ask the important questions: "Where do we go from here? What are we going to do to get there? How are we going to be people who engage in the bigger story and inspire others to be part of that story with us?"

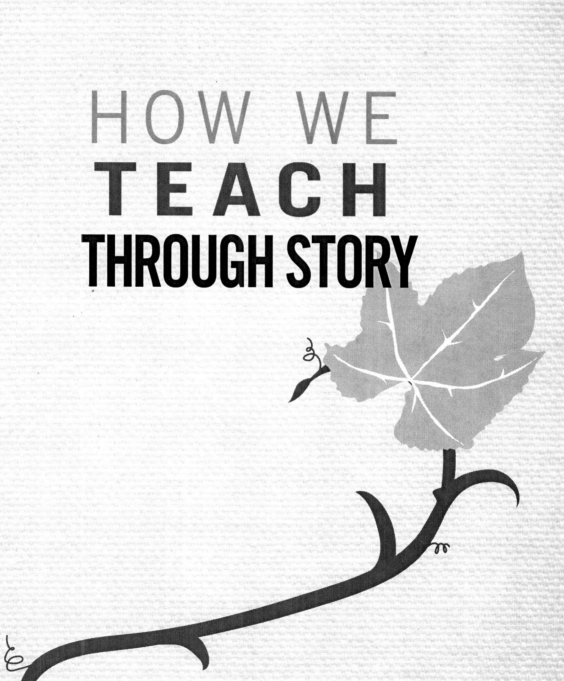

# HOW WE
# TEACH
# THROUGH STORY

# 6

# FINDING A TOPIC

The discussion in this chapter will be affected greatly by your specific capacity as a communicator. As I've mentioned, the art of storytelling is geared toward any communicator, whether it's a schoolteacher, pastor, or anyone serving in a role that requires verbal presentation. For the sake of my area of "expertise," I'll address those of us who are spiritual shepherds (although I believe the forthcoming ideas and strategies can help any communicator discover topics relevant to his or her audience on a number of different levels.)

## "What Life Are We Calling Them to Live?"

I remember standing on the back patio of a buddy's house one beautiful evening with a group of five fellow youth pastors. Every week we had what in large part was my adult "small group." We'd sit around the card table laughing, telling stories, and getting into some heavy theological discussions—my closest friends and me, sharing life together for about four hours. It was the one night of the week I couldn't wait for (and didn't want to end once it arrived).

In fact, more healthy partnerships between youth pastors were born during those times than at any other youth function or youth pastor meeting I'd attended. These weren't rival youth ministers but best friends whom I'd give anything to support, encourage, and partner with. What a beautiful picture.

On this particular night, it was about 9 p.m. We'd finished our game, and we all sat in folding chairs on a four-by-five-foot slab of concrete surrounded by a rotting old fence that had more than its share of patches. For us, the class or quality of the location didn't matter; the people who filled it, however, did. My brother-in-law, Tommy (who was also a youth pastor at that time), began talking. During these gatherings, we'd all throw in our two cents on any given topic. But when Tommy started rolling, we'd just sit back, look at the stars, and listen to him go. This guy was filled with a passion for wrestling with what it looked like to actively live life in the Way of Jesus. He didn't just wax philosophical about what that life might look like; he truly sought to ask the hard questions that might lead to a life reflecting Jesus'. Most of our conversations were pretty raw—and at times they probably wouldn't receive the stamp of approval from most of our church boards. But it was exactly what each of us needed to grow and be effective at what we did.

Tommy continued talking, and he brought up the topic of "calling." Many of us who've been in church circles for any extended amount of time have heard the word *calling* in reference to what God "asks" each of us to do with the lives he's given us. This understanding also suggests that our calling directly relates to the spiritual gifts God's given us. Often it seems we spend more time trying to define *calling* or figure out *our* calling than we do actually living it out.

Tommy then talked about his teenagers and asked us, "What kind of life am I actually calling them to live?" The question stopped all of us in our tracks. Not that we were doing anything else at the time, but we sat in silence as we pondered the question. Then he took it a step further: "You know, I've been thinking, and I have to ask myself if I'm living the kind of life that I'm calling my teenagers to live. I don't want to call them to a life that's theoretical but something to wrestle with and do their best to live out on a daily basis." In his book *The Divine Conspiracy*, Dallas Willard says, "Jesus never called anyone to be a Christian; he only called people to be disciples, individuals who would learn from him and obey all that he commanded."

We can easily take a posture of being "above" the issues we present. "Oh, I remember when I struggled with that when I was a kid." Or "I'll bet this topic is going to bring up some heavy stuff for Timmy or Michelle or Cameron or. . . ." I believe that before we say such things, we need to ask ourselves:

- Is this something I struggle with right now?
- How can I humbly offer myself as one who doesn't have it all together but is willing to work through these issues with my audience?
- Am I willing to allow this issue or topic to bring up the heavy stuff in my own life?

- What are ways that I can call these teenagers to partner *with* me as we take on this cause or live out this teaching of Jesus?

Are we living the kind of lives that we're calling our teenagers to live? Really . . . are we? Do you have your own "small group" with whom you can sit around a table and wrestle with the realities of life and faith? This is a big responsibility, and these are big questions that I believe we must all wrestle with before we move forward in the teaching process.

Now, it goes without saying that no one will ever "nail" this life that we call our teenagers to live. We're all works in progress. But are we actually a work *in progress*—or are we hiding behind the mask of our roles as pastors, teachers, or leaders? It's an easy mask to hide behind, and there are times when I get so good at hiding behind it that I cease to realize that I'm hiding. This can be a scary cycle, and it can lead to disastrous ends. May we be teachers, pastors, and communicators who do our best to partner with others and with God to live out the lives that we're calling our teenagers to live. May we *always* have people in our lives who are permitted to lovingly uncover what may be hidden behind our masks.

## Big Shoes

It's really important that we fully understand and appreciate the opportunity we have to communicate to others. I'm often taken aback when I reflect on the amazing responsibility I've had as the pastor and shepherd to the teenagers in my community. I also think about the stereotypes that surround middle school through college-age youth. Some people will say about my role as a youth pastor, "I feel sorry for you!" or "I remember when I was a kid . . . I sure wouldn't want to be *my* youth pastor!" The comments are endless. And most often they're good spirited (and even very true). But to realize that this "reckless" age group is willing (at least most of the time) to sit in a room and listen to me talk for thirty minutes about the topic of my choice is a HUGE responsibility and a great honor. I'd be surprised if most of their parents have had that opportunity for years!

I know some of our roles differ depending on where you communicate; but no matter the location, you're doing just that—communicating. We have the opportunity to harness the undivided attention of a group of young people for a finite amount of time. We must take such an opportunity seriously; it's our responsibility to take the time and do the research needed in deciding what to talk about.

Hopefully thirty minutes of "teaching time" isn't all we have to communicate a topic. In fact, I'm of the opinion that simply presenting a topic and then assuming the point is being applied in each hearer's life isn't the way to go. So please don't take what I've written about the responsibility of the teacher and believe that I'm saying we're the *only* ones who can bring about change in our kids' lives. Then suddenly we're thinking of ourselves too highly—and that will be reflected in our teaching.

## Practical Suggestions: Personal Exploration, Time, Becoming "Students" of Our Teenagers

### Personal Exploration

My first suggestion for coming up with an effective topic is to choose something that's on your heart. Yes, this can often be draining, discouraging, and downright depressing; but it can also lead to encouragement, profound revelation, and great hope. And I believe it's valuable for helping us grow into more intimate relationships with our Maker.

What topic will you be more passionate about than the one you're personally exploring? When I'm wrestling with a life or faith issue, I tend to put a lot of thought into resolving that issue. It often invades my thoughts at all hours of the day and at the most random times. When I spend intentional time to explore and research, I often come across things that are frustrating, invigorating, or hopeful. Sometimes they're all of those things! So when I'm in the exploration process of an issue that's real to me, I've definitely logged quality time and thought about it. When we prepare to communicate in this way, our teenagers can see that we truly care about what we're presenting. That credibility opens up our listeners to not merely hear our words, but really listen to what we have to say.

Teaching on a topic in which you're personally vested shows vulnerability, which can lead to an atmosphere of partnership, which can lead to active dialogue. We're telling our youth that we're still very much "students" as well. It says that asking questions and seeking answers is not only allowed but is essential to an active faith in Jesus.

In the community of teenagers I serve, I make it very clear that each of them should question what I say to be true and seek out the answers for themselves. As a result of this open and safe atmosphere, most youth are more willing to explore what's being said. They aren't being forced. Of course, my goal is having that gathering place become one of the primary locations to form and develop their answers. And we can do this without forfeiting our leadership role. We each have different definitions of *leadership*. But as we talked about in a previous chapter, we should be leading more as facilitators of the discussion rather than captains of the debate team.

While choosing a topic that's very personal to us can be very effective, don't expect it to be easy. In fact, I've learned from my own experience that it can even be scary. Sometimes we may not have all of the answers or explanations. One may ask, "Doesn't that leave us vulnerable to humiliation?" Well, I believe that really depends on the culture of your teaching setting, and you may need to take that into consideration. But maybe this is when you begin changing the culture of your teaching setting into one that values questions, partnership, and dialogue. It goes back to the question of calling: *What's the faith we want to call our teenagers to live?* Personally, I'd rather risk a knock at my pride and call them to an atmosphere of critical thought, spiritual sensitivity, and great discovery.

## Time

In my experience as a communicator, I've found that it often takes a long time for me to identify a topic that will lead my listeners and me toward lives more closely resembling Jesus'. Obviously, plenty of topics out there deserve our attention, but what's God truly placing on our hearts and minds that we're to communicate to our audience?

Sometimes I believe we just need to let things *marinate*. I'd describe this as an extended amount of time of intentionally seeking one's personal passions and God's direction in one's teaching. This requires time—meaning we may need to create a folder on our computer titled "Marinating Topics" so that whenever we have an experience or revelation, we can take the time to write it down and throw it in the folder. Maybe at some point over the next week or two we'll have another revelation of some kind, and we'll add it to our folders. Subconsciously, our hearts and minds are now looking for ways to identify with these topics in our daily lives. So it may be five months in the works before we finally compile enough stuff to make sense of a topic. This requires awareness and discipline, but it can be a beautiful way of allowing God to slowly work on us—to *marinate* in us, if you will—before we present to our audience.

Of course, to do this means we need to slow down long enough to commune with God. I'm sure we're constantly reminded of and personally convicted of this need (at least I am), but it's essential to our ability to see God's leading clearly. Maybe we need to take a day away from the office and sit on the beach or under a tree and be still. If we look at an interaction Elijah had with God in 1 Kings 19, we see that God didn't speak to Elijah in the wind, fire, or earthquake but in the "still small voice" or "whisper" after all of the commotion had died down. (1 Kings 19:11-13)

What if we also slowed down and got out of the commotion for a while? What if we asked God where he wants us to lead and direct our youth in their faith? We've been given great responsibility to lead, shepherd, and pastor our young people. Where do our personal convictions meet God's call on us to lead them? We need time to gain understanding. The reality is that *we do* all have the time. Let's commit to allowing ourselves enough time to *marinate* in the leadings of our Creator.

## Becoming "Students" of Our Teenagers

One of my favorite stereotypes of youth pastors is that we're "adult kids" who wear high-top L.A. Gear tennis shoes, sport extra puffy Hammer pants, and say things like "hang loose" and "bodacious." And yes, we're all probably picturing one youth pastor in our town who still dresses like that (and he probably has a better heart than the rest of us!). But I find it ironic that people often think we have to dress like that in order to be "relevant" to our youth. First off, if that style of dress were *ever* relevant, it was two decades ago. Plus, I don't necessarily believe our young people are looking for adults who are mirror images of them.

In order to communicate to teenagers in a way that leads to active conversation and formative relationships, we must know where they're at and what they're wrestling with. The reason I bring up the "Hammer pants youth pastor" illustration is because I don't believe youth are looking for leaders who try to be "cool"; they're looking for leaders who are willing to ask hard questions and seek honest answers. They don't want or need entertainment as much as they want or need places to openly evaluate the realities of life.[3] (Some teenagers may not even realize this about themselves.)

---

3. Rob Bell, teaching pastor of Mars Hill in Grand Rapids, gave a very insightful talk titled, "Everything Is Spiritual." It's worth picking up on DVD.

Our role should be more or less "tour guides" of faith rather than scientists who only present hard data. Teenagers need adults to shepherd them on their journeys toward spiritual maturity. And by "spiritual maturity" I don't just mean their theological understandings but their understanding that all of life is spiritual.[4] We need to avoid compartmentalizing our lives into tidy categories.

As I mentioned earlier in this book, my wife and I have been in Costa Rica for five weeks. The trip is coming to an end, but we've done our best to keep in email contact with our friends and family. One of our teenagers emailed us four days ago. She wrote a very honest, brave note that included some things she's been wrestling with since we've been gone. But one thing I noticed was that she evaluated how "good" she was doing based on different categories of her life. For example, she wrote that things with her family and friends were going well, but her spiritual life was not going "good" at all. She hadn't been to church since we left, and she couldn't remember the last time she'd prayed or read the Bible. I completely understand what she was trying to say, and I often come into this compartmentalizing mindset as well. So my wife and I responded to her beautiful email by encouraging her to see *all* of life as her spiritual life.

But if we claim to be in relationship with Jesus every hour of every day, wouldn't that mean that every hour of every day encompasses our spiritual lives? It's as though each of our lives is a mosaic, and each "category" is a different piece of a larger, more beautiful image. Therefore, it's important that we look at our lives as "working mosaics" as opposed to individual pieces of art that can be evaluated on their own. For instance, are we honoring God not only in how or when we read the Bible, but also in how we interact with and love those around us? Or in what we choose to do with our friends? Do we slow down long enough to have a conversation with that homeless fellow who sits on our street corner *every* day, or do we simply drive by him once we realize we don't have any granola bars in our car?

We must be "students" to the teenagers we're communicating with— those we've been called to serve. We serve them by understanding where they're at and doing our best to lovingly challenge them forward into an understanding that sees every aspect of life as spiritual.

There are a few ways we can be active "students" of our teenagers. We can do our best to understand the culture they live in, we can ask them

---

4. *A New Kind of Youth Ministry.*

lots of questions, and we can reflect on past conversations and experiences we've had with them.

First, I think of my wife. She's a pop-culture diva. Ask her about any up-and-coming indie band, and she probably already has them on her iPod. She usually knows the basics of the latest movies and musicians, but they don't consume her. She's found a balance between unhealthy obsession and complete cultural isolation. Some would disagree with me here, and I can understand the perspective that says we don't need to waste time on the shallowness of pop culture. But when I see my wife talking, laughing, and building credibility with the very teen who's ignored me for six months—and does it through a conversation about the eye makeup of a lead singer—I have to believe there can be great value in this understanding. We can have a grasp of pop culture without promoting it in an unhealthy way.

Second, I believe it's important to ask *a lot* of questions—not only of our teenagers, but of anyone who may give us some insight into the world our young people live in. It's easy for us to believe we have all the answers or to find ourselves doing most of the talking in our relationships with our youth—but it's crucial that we don't do this. In the same way that we ask our teenagers to be active listeners, we need to be active listeners regarding their lives and the world around them. When you slow down long enough to hear a story or two, it's pretty overwhelming to know what this generation's dealing with.

Finally, we need to take time to reflect on past conversations and experiences with our teens. We need to process. Often I've found that the topic I'm looking for has been brought up frequently during my conversations with youth, but I hadn't taken the time to process what was said. If they're the ones we're trying to reach, then don't be surprised if they hold the answers to our topic searches. (This goes back to our conversation on the use of time. Some intentional time spent examining the context and content of our conversations and experiences with our teenagers is very important, whether or not it leads to a story topic.)

## Jesus' Higher Calling

My wife and I have been studying the Sermon on the Mount with a group of close friends. We've broken it down into seven sections, and we read one section each day of the week. Having gone through it a few times now, it's interesting to understand the message that Jesus is bringing to his audience. He speaks to each of us with a higher calling; in fact, throughout much of the sermon he uses the phrase, "You have heard that it was said . . . but I tell you." Each example leads to a greater understanding and calling to not only live out previous teachings, but also to step up to a whole new way of life that revolves around the example of Jesus.

Here are a few excerpts from Matthew 5 NIV:

> **21** *"You have heard that it was said* to the people long ago, 'Do not murder, and anyone who murders will be subject to judgment.' **22** *But I tell you* that anyone who is angry with his brother will be subject to judgment."

> **27** *"You have heard that it was said,* 'Do not commit adultery.' **28** *But I tell you* that anyone who looks at a woman lustfully has already committed adultery with her in his heart."

> **33** *"Again, you have heard that it was said* to the people long ago, 'Do not break your oath, but keep the oaths you have made to the Lord.' **34** *But I tell you,* Do not swear at all: either by heaven, for it is God's throne; **35** or by the earth, for it is his footstool; or by Jerusalem, for it is the city of the Great King."

> **38** *"You have heard that it was said,* 'Eye for eye, and tooth for tooth.' **39** *But I tell you,* Do not resist an evil person. If someone strikes you on the right cheek, turn to him the other also."[5]

It's almost as though Jesus is saying, "Okay, the way things used to work I affirm as true, but . . ." And then he continues, "If we're to be active participants in God's story—his mission to put things back to the way they were originally intended—then we must live out an even higher calling." The more I read and study the Sermon on the Mount, the more I realize how radical Jesus' message really is. I'm drawn to his passion for creating change in the world now. I'm blown away by his vast understanding of the context he finds himself in. But more than anything, I see that Jesus isn't content settling for an apathetic and disengaged life of faith. He wants more. He expects more. And it's our role as communicators of this message to present Jesus' higher calling to our young people through word and deed.

We've discussed how to come up with a topic, but now it's time to evaluate whether it's what Jesus would have us teach. Are we calling our young people forward? Are we willing to look at Jesus' message of a higher calling and communicate that (with hope) to our teenagers? Are we giving them examples of what that could look like? Are *we* the example?

---

5. See Glen Stassen and David Gushee's insightful argument for a threefold or triadic pattern within this passage in *Kingdom Ethics*, 135–40.

## Practical Application

- Take time to articulate some of the issues you're personally exploring and wrestling with.

- Create a "Marinating Topics" folder on your computer.

- Take time to slow down and commune with God by listening to his "whispers."

- Make an intentional effort to be a better "student" of your teenagers.

- Evaluate whether or not you're encouraging your students to live out Jesus' higher calling.

*7*

# CREATING A STORY WITH SETTING, CHARACTERS, AND A PLOT

## *Agada* Time

If you're taking the art of storytelling seriously, then it's time to begin creating your story based on the principles that the ancient Jewish rabbis used when they created Jewish *agada* to illuminate God's message. The Hebrew word for "parable" is *mashal*—a proverbial saying, prophetic figurative discourse, or sentence of ethical wisdom. The Jewish rabbi wouldn't take this art of prophetic discourse lightly. These stories weren't designed to articulate mundane or static principles. While the Old Testament doesn't contain many parables, Jesus—a first-century rabbi—taught through them consistently. Jesus most often used them to illuminate his central message of the new inaugurated Kingdom of God. Their importance is emphasized in Proverbs 26:7: "The legs of the lame are not equal: so [is] a parable (*mashal*) in the mouth of fools." Parables can sound elementary, but they point to the sacred—illuminating something true of human nature and/or the divine.

Where to start? A key place is by telling contextually relevant stories to our audiences. There are numerous definitions of *contextualization*, but one I find most helpful is from Latin American theologian René Padilla:

> To contextualize the gospel is so to translate it that the Lordship of Jesus Christ is not an abstract principle or a mere doctrine, but the determining factor of all of life in all its dimensions and the basic criterion in relation to which all the cultural values that form the very substance of human life are evaluated. Without contextualization the gospel will become tangential or even entirely irrelevant.

*(Mission Between the Times, 93)*

At one point in the apostle Paul's ministry, he found himself speaking to a Jewish audience in Antioch (Acts 13). So he presented the gospel message as the fulfillment of Old Testament prophecy, with Jesus as a true descendant of David. Later Paul speaks in Athens at the Areopagus and, through his understanding of Greek thought, presents Jesus' message using the "idol to an unknown god" to open the minds of his audience (Acts 17:16–34).

A chart found in a very insightful book by Alan Hirsch and Michael Frost called *The Shaping of Things to Come* offers a visual of Paul's use of contextualization (85).

| Topic | Antioch | Athens |
|---|---|---|
| God | Covenant Lord of Israel | Transcendent/Immanent Creator |
| Humanity | Has rejected the promised Son of David | Has wrongly depicted the Creator by a portion of creation |
| Jesus | Son of David/Son of God | The risen judge |
| Response | Welcome the Gospel | Turn from worship of idols |
| Promise | Forgiveness of sin | Escape the coming wrath |

As communicators, we must physically and mentally place ourselves where our audiences experience life. We need to think about all of the elements of the world around them. Jesus' message can be understood in every context, but our ability to speak *through* the context of our listeners offers them greater clarity and understanding.

## Picturing Each Young Person's Face and Story

We have our topics established; now it's time to attach legs to our stories. Our minds are open to every option available to us while looking through the lens of the main message we're working to convey. It's this work of assembling the pieces—topic, context, theology—into a rich mosaic that makes this one of the *artistic* aspects of teaching through storytelling. As we contemplate our stories, we need to picture the faces and stories of each of our young people.

- Picture Katey . . .
- How about Timmy . . .

- Josh . . .

- Jason . . .

- Now Jennifer . . .

- And Sarah . . .

What are their stories? What's going on in their lives? What activities are they interested in? Where do they live? What are their family dynamics? What are their thoughts on God? Are they lonely and isolated from the world? Are they captains of their football teams or school princesses? Do they have all the "Christian" answers? What has your personal interaction been like with each one of them? Why do they come to your gathering? Are they judgmental toward others? Do they smile when nobody's looking? Are they often angry? If so, do you know what drives their anger? The list goes on and on and on . . .

The story you're creating is designed to convey a message and start a conversation among *them*: The kid whose mom just died in a car accident; the one who was crowned MVP of his baseball team; or the youth who wears black eye makeup, has numerous piercings, and seems more interested in his iPod playlist than anything you have to say. These are our teenagers. At *every* point in the story-creation process, we must picture these faces and stories so we can fully connect the stories we create with the stories of their lives. And we must ask ourselves, *How can this story speak to them right where they are?*

> "The first and most obvious characteristic of fiction is that it deals with reality through what can be seen, heard, smelt, tasted and touched."
> Flannery O'Connor, *Mystery and Manners* (New York: Farrar, Straus & Giroux, 1961)

## Preaching to Just One Teen

In going through this process of picturing each young person's story and doing our best to speak to that, it's easy to fall into the habit of preaching to one specific teenager. Most often it's the youth who's found his way under your skin for some reason, and now you believe it's your time to "tell" him how wrong he is. We may begin to think, *I'm going to tell you what's been on my mind for a LONG time.* I plead with you to think otherwise.

I remember preparing a story that dealt with the topics of legalism and being judgmental before allowing ourselves to fully love and understand those we're unfairly evaluating. The story dealt with everything from how we read the Bible to how we present Jesus' message to those around us. Well, in my preparation of the story, I—subconsciously—began preaching (through a specific character in the story) to one teenager. This young person came off as the know-it-all and acted as though he had all the world's problems figured out. Any opinion that differed from his was unacceptable to him. Those who know me best know that this mentality brings me to premature aging. It turns me into the very person I'm frustrated with! (I obviously have many issues of my own . . . )

Anyway, throughout my story I was speaking in large part to this one teenager. Without even realizing it, I was telling myself that I'd put him in his place. I'd guilt him into thinking the "right" way. As I began delivering my story to the teenagers, it hit me hard: I was preaching to only *one* of them. And I wasn't preaching in a loving way, either; I was preaching in a judgmental way. Rather than connecting the young people's stories to God's story, my story simply became about *me*.

This goes back to the mentality of this chance to preach as being "our" time. It's absolutely a time for speaking to the specific issues involved in each young person's life. It's also when we're given the honor of presenting an idea or truth to the young people we believe that God put on our hearts for a reason. Good stuff.

That said, when we take this tack of "teaching" the group and instead begin "preaching" to one or two helpless teenagers, we're missing the mark. We're being irresponsible and immature leaders. It becomes about us. And it's obvious not just to the teens we're preaching to, but to everyone. The other teenagers can sense you're on a personal rant that's grounded in arrogance and retribution instead of in love. Bad stuff.

## Basic Outline

Before you begin creating and developing your setting, characters, and plot, it's important that you first come up with a basic outline—what I call a "skeleton story." A skeleton story is the foundation offering you an understanding in how the setting, character, and plot details move you and your audience toward your main point. It consists of the preliminary "bullet points" of your story.

When you create your skeleton story, as with all aspects in your story creation, I suggest you find a comfortable place that inspires creativity. Comfort and inspiration are found in different places for all of us. Whatever your choice, consider that location and go there.

First, you need to come up with the basic information—where the story takes place, the primary characters, and the plot. If you haven't already decided on a central biblical passage, now's the time to establish the biblical basis for your story. One of your characters can bring it up, or you may choose it as the foundation for your story and discuss it in your follow-up conversation.

Your basic plot will contain character and storyline development, conflict(s), a climax, and a resolution. You're an artist who's beginning to create a beautiful work (even though you may not think so at first!) in order to convey a rich message that engages each teenager's story on myriad levels.

From my experience, this is the time when it's easiest to have a serious brain freeze. All of your preparation, research, and Spirit-led convictions are coming to you all at once, and maybe you won't know where to start. Or the opposite may be true: You've put in the legwork, and now you can't see any connection between your work and the proposed story. My advice is simply to begin writing—maybe bullet points, maybe manuscript, just come up with something. I believe you'll be surprised at how things will come to you once you put pen to paper . . . or fingers to keyboard.

This said, the skeleton story is *not* designed as the finished product; it's only a guide to jump-start your thinking and vision for the story. And you must be willing to add, subtract, or throw away much of it, if necessary. It's a work in progress, and a lot of it may not even make sense once you've further developed your setting, characters, and plot.

## Practical Application

- Write your topic at the top of a blank sheet of paper or computer screen.

- Underneath that, write the words SETTING, CHARACTERS, SCRIPTURE PASSAGE, and PLOT in a vertical list. Follow each word with a colon and leave plenty of space between each one.

- Develop and fill in the basic information for each section. Do your "Plot" section last and allow it to be a continuing series of bullet points down your page. Hopefully this allows for a fluid train of thought as you create.

Remember: You're still picturing the faces and stories of your young people.

## Setting

It's now time to create and develop the setting with your basic understanding of the skeleton story. The setting isn't just the physical location within the story; it's the characteristics of that location. For example, let's say the primary setting of your story takes place at a high school. Where exactly is the school located? What surrounds it? What is the school known for? What are the demographics within the school? Is it known as a school for jocks, or musicians, or skaters, and so on? Is it a Christian school? Such questions about the characteristics of your primary location could go on and on and on. That noted, it's important for us to have thought through those kinds of questions. As storytellers, we need as much credibility as we can get. Presenting a well-thought-out setting goes a long way toward establishing that credibility.

You might feel as though I've already overemphasized the idea of understanding your audience. But once again, we run into its importance. Contextualization (as we discussed earlier in this chapter) is essential to the message we send through our choice of setting. The setting should be marked by characteristics your youth have either experienced or are familiar with. This allows your teenagers to actively visualize and be a part of the setting as you tell the story.

Looking again at Jesus' parable of the prodigal son (see the end of chapter 1), we might note that it was set in a Jewish land that practiced Jewish traditions. When the younger son runs away, there's a clear understanding that when he enters a "foreign" land, he's no longer in that Jewish setting. The rules change. Jesus' audience would immediately identify with the characteristics of both settings. They understood the culture and context, so he didn't have to reteach what was unique to both settings. In the same way that Jesus fully understood his story's setting, we must be prepared to explain the significance of the setting we choose.

Another possibility is choosing a setting that's been part of your personal experience. Whether it's the cul-de-sac where you grew up or the local ball field where you played Little League, a familiar location affords greater detail. It also allows you to improvise as you tell the story, which I believe is very important. You can go into a detailed description of a park bench you sat on with your dad on Saturdays, or the ice cream shop you and your buddies went to every day in the summer. Of course these details are supposed to be a part of your character's story, not your own. Vivid, true-to-life detail builds credibility with your audience as well.

## Practical Application

- Write a one- or two-word description of the primary setting at the top of a blank sheet of paper or computer screen.

- Underneath it, create three columns across the page labeled: CHARACTERISTICS, PERSONAL DETAILS, and ALTERNATE SETTINGS. (These are locations other than your primary one. If you want to get really detailed, you could make a similar sheet for each one of them.)

- Fill out all three columns and keep them visible throughout the rest of the creation of the story.

Remember: You're still picturing the faces and stories of your young people.

## Characters

I see the characters as the primary carriers of the main messages we're hoping to communicate. In a well-created and well-delivered story, our characters' stories become our young people's stories, too. They're walking and talking illustrations of the message we're working so hard to convey. The characters come to life as their stories are told. And our youth are so captivated by these stories the characters are telling, they can't help but see the characters as a reflection of themselves on some level. For all of these reasons, quality and thorough character development is essential to an effective story.

Since it's crucial to speak to our audiences, obviously the characters should be believable to them. Our character choices greatly reflect our understanding of our audiences—and how much credibility we hope to gain as a result.

A basic rule is to create characters in the same life stage as the hearer, since different age groups deal with different issues. Most middle schoolers, for example, aren't so concerned about the complexities, anxieties, and uncertainties of graduating from high school and trying to figure out what to do with their lives. Those issues are way off their radars.

I'll often tell the same basic story to our middle schoolers and high schoolers, but I'll change the setting, characters, and, to some degree, the plot. It can be as simple as making sure your characters are thirteen years old instead of seventeen years old, or at times the age difference may require a whole different story. Ultimately it's up to the storytellers—equipped with a working knowledge of their listeners' life situations—to make the necessary adjustments.

It's also important to have a clear understanding of each character's role within the bigger message of the story *before* the story is presented. There are a few basics to character creation and development that are essential for every facet of your story to play out in the rich ways that you intend them to. I'll offer some basic insights into the roles of the main character(s), supporting character(s), and what I call the fringe character(s).

## Main Character

The main character is the person we're telling the story *through* who's affecting (or affected by) most aspects of the story's plot (character development, conflict, climax, and resolution). For this reason this character needs thorough development and believable attributes, should reflect the story's setting, must be a conduit for your main point coming to life, and should be rooted in an understanding of your audience.

If we go way back to our analysis of the prodigal son parable, we see the father as the main character Jesus chose to convey his primary message. Jesus tells his audience this story *through* the father. We see how the father can be compared to God the Father and is a reflection of a God who offers free will and grace to the undeserving.

The father is also central to two subplots in this story: First, the older brother rebels against his father by viewing him as merely a boss who pays his wages, which blocks the older brother from the traditional role as family peacemaker. Further he fails to forgive his younger brother, while the father is more than willing to do so. Second, the younger brother also rebels by viewing his father as a source of income and then running away and wasting his inheritance. Again, *through* the character of the father, Jesus illuminates his message of God the Father as a God of endless grace, mercy, and understanding, while offering his people free will.

Get as detailed as possible with character qualities, too, by creating a detailed character sheet. It should include your main character's name, the primary message the character is designed to convey, family history, interests, friends, school information, and so on. Don't edit yourself here. Use your artful mind to create a main character with a story that's full of life and details—in the same way your teenagers' stories are full of life and details. Your goal is for your audience to not only understand this character, but also *know* this character. Most likely, this will be the one character's story that your youth remember six months, a year, or two years down the road.

## Supporting Character(s)

I see the supporting character's main role as illuminating your primary message through her interaction with the main character, whether in a positive (protagonist) or negative (antagonist) way. We must embrace the fact that the most effective supporting character may be an antagonist. Our teenagers can relate to difficult people and ugly situations. In fact I'd argue that most of them have people in their lives who antagonize them consistently, and they don't know healthy ways to respond.

In the parable of the prodigal son, we see two supporting characters: The older brother and the younger brother. Through each brother's story, the audience sees many different ways that people can rebel against a gracious and caring God. Some may relate more to the older brother's story, while others may relate to the younger brother's. But both stories enhance the power and clarity of the father's story. Individually, their stories were unique, powerful, and pointed; but they weren't created to stand alone. They didn't make the point that Jesus was seeking to make until they tied back into the dynamic story of the father.

As with the main character, I suggest creating a supporting character sheet that gives context and insight. It may not need as much detail as the main character's sheet. Nonetheless, it should contain basic information that will create greater clarity, understanding, and credibility.

## Fringe Characters

They don't have large roles in the story, but their roles are profoundly essential nonetheless. They are mediums to communicate your main point to your audience in a believable and fluid manner, adding to your story's credibility, understanding, and purpose. They're characters whose names show up more than halfway down a cast list at the end of a movie. In other words, they're probably not recognizable celebrity names, yet they're still essential to the telling of a rich and compelling story.

A few fringe characters that come to mind in the parable of the prodigal son are the pig farmer in the "foreign land" and the servants at the father's estate. Although they have very little "camera time," they add depth and richness to the story. The pig farmer tells the audience that the younger brother is in a land of Gentiles, which is significant to a mixed (Jewish and Gentile) audience and illustrates the depravity of the son's situation (Luke 15:15). The servants who respond to the father's request to take care of his younger son tell the audience that the father still has some authority over his estate even after he'd divided it between his two sons (Luke 15:22). These characters add to the plot, enhance the characters with larger roles, and are evidence of Jesus' understanding of the story's context.

I don't believe a full character sheet is necessary for each of your fringe characters. My only suggestion is that you understand who these characters are before you deliver your story. Be strategic regarding where you place them in your story—not to simply add a character, but to add richness to the story as a whole.

Remember: You're still picturing the faces and stories of your young people.

## Practical Application

- Create character sheets for both your main character(s) and supporting character(s). Include their name(s); the main message they're used to convey; and a detailed list of their characteristics, interests, and backgrounds.

- Make a list of the fringe characters. Give them strategic roles that enhance the richness of your story.

# Plot

Now it's time to develop a detailed plot line for your story. At this point you already have a skeleton story with the basic plot information in place. You've also developed your setting and characters. Is it now necessary for you to alter your basic plot to better utilize your setting and characters to more effectively illustrate your main point? I hope it's become clear that the creation of the story is a beautiful and extremely artful experience. The setting, characters, and plot don't exist independently of each other; they're woven together like a beautiful, powerful vine. Each element of the story must feed and build off the others, leading us to a dynamic masterpiece. In many ways, the plot isn't merely the glue holding the other elements together; it's the driving force that brings to light the powerful message through the marriage of each element to the others.

Do your best to get a visual for the story as a *whole* while taking into account your skeleton story, setting, and characters. Where do you want this to go? What message do you want to make exceedingly clear? Maybe you want your primary message to be hidden—like many of the messages within Jesus' parables—so they're more powerful when they're finally discovered and applied by a perceptive audience.

This is the time to make those decisions and play them out through the actions of your characters. I recommend going back to the skeleton story and creatively describing each step the main character takes toward resolution. Of course that will lead you into the actions of your supporting and fringe characters as they complement the main character's journey. You don't want your plot to unwrap but rather to thoughtfully unfold.

Picture Christmas morning when kids unwrap their presents with no other intention except to get to the grand finale—the contents inside. There's no rhythm or consideration of what it took to create the paper, the intricacies of each fold, or the thought put into it. It's all about what's inside. When we create our plot, however, we want it to unfold in an intentional and formative way. We want to enjoy and participate in the process of the story coming to life. Our plot shouldn't be designed just for the high-profile finish but to illuminate the spiritually saturated truths being brought to light as it unfolds.

For some, simply creating bullet points of the plot could work. However you feel best equipped to add thought, creativity, and allow the Spirit's leading is the route you should take. I would suggest writing down *everything*. Even if it sounds ridiculous or out of place at the time, write it down. You can always go back and edit, but you don't want to ignore an idea that may enhance the richness of your story.

Once you've created and written down a detailed plot, I'd suggest reading it through the lens of the main point you're working to communicate to your audience. Does this plot create a medium for your topic to come to life and lead to authentic questions and discussion? Does your story contain the essential content you'd originally planned on using to teach and grow your youth?

Carefully walk through your manuscript and make sure your plot is leading toward your main topic at every point. Further, ensure that it's backed with the Scripture you thought to be appropriate and theologically clear. It's easy to create a whole story and then realize it's simply a subjective piece of personal propaganda. Take the time to critically examine your intentions and use the content of your research to give your story a foundation.

Remember: You're still picturing the faces and stories of your young people.

## Practical Application
- Write down a comprehensive manuscript of your story from start to finish. You may want to break it up according to scenes so it's easier to visualize each transition. This will also help with clarity when you're delivering the story.

- I'd suggest creating another plot script (same plot), only in bullet points. This contains less detail, but it's easier to teach from and may encourage spontaneity and creativity when you're presenting it. You've written the whole story, so it's already in your head—just trust that it is!

## We All Can Be Artists!
All the descriptions and suggestions in this chapter are based on my personal experience. I fully understand that each of us works differently and has insights that could enhance the story creation. Please view these pages as a helpful guidebook, not a detailed procedure manual. If done differently, the world isn't going to cave in and no one will die. Chances are it'll be better than if you do it exactly the way I describe here because it will be more true to you as an artist. That said, please feel comfortable to use every sug-

gestion or simply pull a few that could be helpful to you. My hope is that the discussion in this chapter has, at the very least, opened up a way for each of us to release the God-given creativity and passion he's placed within us to love and serve our teenagers through the art of storytelling.

# 8

# DELIVERING A STORY

## Something Worth Telling

From the ages of ten to eighteen, golf was the center of my life. I played every day in the summer and every weekend during the school year with my best buddy, Travis. From the moment I picked up my first golf club, I knew I wanted to be a professional golfer.

I worked at the local golf course so I could play for free, and I ended up playing my first year of college golf for one of the best teams in the state. How I played on the course meant a lot to me.

On one very windy afternoon at the local municipal course, I was playing with Travis and an older couple who'd joined up with us at the turn (that's the tenth hole in golf lingo). I wasn't having my best day, but I was still having a good time, as always. The next several holes were uneventful—until the seventeenth hole, 131 yards away from the tee. Since the wind was gusting in our faces, I decided to hit a lower shot that would stay under the wind. There was some glare around the green, so it was hard to see the flag inside the hole. But I had the basic location in mind and stepped up to the tee after everyone else had hit. I went through my usual routine and settled in to take my swing. The ball contact wasn't my best, but I remember seeing the ball headed straight toward what I thought was the flagpole. It stayed low under the wind like I was hoping, and it bounced about 25 feet in front of the pin.

At this point Travis, the older couple, and I were all silent as we watched with anticipation. I thought to myself, *There's no way this could actually happen.* The ball rolled upon the green, and as best as we could tell (because of the glare), it looked like the ball dropped into the hole! None of us were certain it went in, so we didn't do too much celebrating yet. But I ran up to the green like a giddy schoolboy (which I was). My golf ball was nowhere to be seen, so I went straight to the hole—and there it was! I did it! A hole in one! We all started cheering, and I got some high-fives. All was well in the universe, and now I had a story I wanted to tell *everyone*.

When we as communicators finally get to the place where we're able to tell a story, it's important that we *want* to tell it. We put a lot of time into the creation process, did the research, and now we have a message burning in hearts that we want to share with others. Our attitude should reflect excitement and anticipation to share something powerful—something leading to greater depths of conversation and spiritual maturity among our teenagers. We've come to something beautiful, and we want to share every part of it with others. Our young people can tell when we're excited to share something and when we're simply talking at them because that's our job.

If we aren't excited to tell our stories, why should anyone be excited to hear them? By "excited" I don't mean a cheesy, artificial excitement. In fact some stories are extremely heavy and won't lead you to a "happy" excited but a divine anticipation for the potential of great change in your teenagers' lives. That's still a form of excitement, but obviously it's not the kind that leads you to don your clown nose and juggle flaming knives. (Actually, I'm not sure if that reflects excitement or just weirdness . . . )

One way for the audience to catch your excitement is through your ability to tell your story as if you're "there." If you can picture yourself in the story, you may be surprised at the detail and believability that's added when you tell it. A firsthand recollection of an experience is always more exciting to listen to than a third- or fourth-hand version. Put yourself into the story and let it come to life.

I'd also suggest that as you tell your story, you should believe in its effectiveness. Know that you've put in the time and heart and have allowed the Spirit to lead you to this point. Don't stop in the middle of the story and insert a self-deprecating comment such as, "I know this is dumb," or "I don't know what I was thinking when I came up with this." At the end of the story, when you're in a time of discussion, maybe you can offer that one particular part of the story wasn't as realistic as you would've liked it to be, but it was created that way to make a point.

This isn't a blanket statement, but in large part I believe your story will be as effective and rich as *you* believe it to be. So allow yourself to leave your comfort zone and trust that God will honor your attitude through the changed lives of your teens.

## Where Did That Come From?

Everybody uses notes differently. Some of us like to have every word scripted out, some like bullet points, and others don't use notes at all. And I know there are numerous ways to organize your notes between each of those styles. Whatever your comfort level, I suggest that you lean as much as you can toward the "noteless" end of the spectrum. I realize the idea of speaking in front of an audience "without a net" is more terrifying than going pantless in front of an audience (for some of us, anyway). Again, I'm not saying you must go noteless, but I am suggesting that if you're a manuscript person, then you might work toward using a modified bullet-point version . . . and so on.

My reason is simple: Even though some of us would say God skipped us when he handed out the gift of creativity (in fact, my best man used his entire wedding speech to tell everyone how incredibly *un*creative I am), I DO believe we all have some creativity in us. And, in my opinion, the biggest reason we may assume that we don't is because we haven't tried to experiment in new ways that would test our creativity. If we don't have every detail of our stories written down, then to some degree we're forced to add the details as we go. By the time you're ready to deliver your story, you've most likely put in the necessary amounts of thought and time to write it out. So now it's time to trust that you *know* your story. And if there's a hole or two in the telling of it, just fill those spots with some spontaneous creativity.

If this is still a terrifying proposition for you, try locking yourself in a room and then tell your story with very few notes and see how you do. Work on filling in the holes with appropriate, creative content. We must remember that we're not giving a propositional, three-point sermon. We're presenting a work of art that's forced us to feel, listen, hear, and fully experience the story we're telling.

## Leave Them Wanting More

A great way to keep your young people's attention is by ending a section of the story with a cliff-hanger. I'm sure many of us have watched TV shows that have us completely hooked when we suddenly realize that with only two minutes left in the episode, there's just too much story left to tell. Then the brutal words TO BE CONTINUED . . . flash on the screen. I'm usually frustrated for a little while, but then I'm anxiously awaiting the rest of the story next week. I'm proposing the same concept for our stories with youth.

Of course, not all teens will be so engaged in your story that they'll anxiously await the continuation—but some will. Considering our typical teenage audience, knowing that *any* young person will be excited to hear what you have to say the next week is a beautiful thing! It's not uncommon for a sad-faced teenager to approach me after "story time" and say, "I'm not going to be here next week, so I don't know how I'm going to hear what happens next!" I usually respond by encouraging the teen to ask one of her friends who *can* make it the next week. That response can be a little risky, but teaching this way allows for that to occur.

In the days before I taught through story, teenagers rarely remembered exactly what we'd discussed the week before. But teaching through story allows youth to catch up their friends on whatever they missed because they're simply remembering a story in order to access the content. As we discussed in chapter 3, the mind can better retain and process information presented in this way than many other modes of communication.

## Take It Easy

As we tell our stories, it's really important that we don't get mechanical. It's easy to do this when we're trying to remember every piece of information we've prepared—character traits, settings, plotlines, important Bible passages, and so on. There's no need to stress out if you miss a point or two. The story will continue, and in most cases the impact won't be compromised. The worst-case scenario is that you may have to clarify or add something during the follow-up discussion time. This leads me to my next point.

## Conversation

Often the most formative and positive revelations come during the post-story conversation, which is designed to be a time of rich questioning, dialogue, and exposition. It should be an open forum for authenticity.

This isn't to say that the impact of a Spirit-led story can't bring about positive life change in and of itself. If we look at Jesus' teaching through Jewish *agada*, there were numerous times when he wouldn't offer his personal insights and application of the story. But that didn't stop the disciples and other listeners from discussing the content and meaning. Even so I believe the impact of the story's message will be greater if followed by some form of honest dialogue.

If we look at early examples of our faith, it was part of their spiritual ethos to seek out the truths of Scripture in community. God created us to live and grow in the setting of *community*. We have the opportunity as shepherds of our kids to facilitate and guide such conversation that may lead to profound life change.

For these reasons, it's important that we prepare discussion questions. We need to take the time not only to jot down a few questions, but also formulate questions filled with intention that lead our teenagers toward the primary message we're working to convey. It's been established that this message has been geared for the ears and hearts of our audience; we've sought God's leading and have been a "student" of our young people; and we've concluded that this is the message they need to hear and act upon. Therefore, we must guide our questions and discussion toward that original leading, while at the same time leaving room for other questions the Spirit may lead our teens to ask.

Further, it's not essential to have answers for all the questions that come up. There may be instances when we need to do some preparation for questions that surface, but I'd focus on facilitating a discussion that brings youth to a place where they can come up with the answers themselves. Or sometimes they may have to live in the highly spiritual tension that involves not knowing all the answers. Lead them forward in critical conversation—don't just spout out answers as though it's your duty as the leader. More processing, which often leads to deeper issues and more profound insights, may be necessary.

Something that's enhanced and added depth to our post-story conversations is leaving a whole teaching time solely for reflection and application. As I've mentioned, each week we usually have twenty to thirty minutes of discussion after a portion of the story is told. This discussion time is great but often incomplete. As a result we often take an entire week's gathering, following completion of the story, to break off into smaller groups and process. This dynamic allows leaders to pursue follow-up and offers a more intentional time of deconstructing the story and its main storylines. Further, it offers more time and opportunity for an open forum, which can be important for young people who may not otherwise bring up points in a larger group setting with less time.

More than anything, I've been grateful for the relational follow-up and practical application that have come as a result of this extended dialogue. It requires that all leaders be on the same page, which may take some additional leadership on your part. But it's well worth the effort.

## Practical Application

- Based on your comfort level, take one tangible step toward going "noteless."

- Give your story a practice run with very few notes or none at all.

- In your final teaching outline, be sure to leave room for Spirit-led creativity.

- Do your best to present the story as if you are (or were) there. Don't stress about occasionally missing a point.

- Prepare intentional discussion questions that move the conversation forward toward your intended message.

- Consider devoting an entire week's gathering to a time of reflection, conversation, and application of the story.

# MY MANUSCRIPT
## STORIES
## BY TOPIC

*Feel Free to Copy and Paste!*

# 9

# JIMMY AND DAVID

*Topics—Participating and Serving in the Kingdom of God, Repentance, Outreach, Mercy, Forgiveness, Friendship*

## Part I: What a Life!

Jimmy and David were the best of friends. They grew up on the same street at the end of a cul-de-sac. Their town was very nice with lots of people who looked a lot like they did and knew each other's names.

Both Jimmy and David's parents had lived in this town since the boys were born, so it was all the boys knew. They loved it there and felt as though life couldn't be lived any better than they were living it.

Jimmy and David first met when they were five years old. It was actually because their parents forced them to hang out. Their parents got along with each other, and living so close, they wanted to make sure Jimmy and David became friends at an early age so they'd each have a good buddy nearby. At first they really didn't like each other and didn't know what to talk about. Because Jimmy loved to play sports and David was more into Legos and action heroes, they spent most of their time playing video games. But the more time they spent together, the closer they got. With each passing year, Jimmy and David became harder to separate.

Although Jimmy and David didn't mind going to school because it meant they could see each other and their other buddies every day, they definitely preferred the summer. This time of the year meant sunshine, running through the sprinklers, eating all kinds of junk food, and LOTS of time for video games. In fact they'd each save all the money they could in order to buy as many new video games as possible. Most every day either Jimmy or David would call the other one.

"Hey, Jimmy, what are you doing today?" David asked.

"Nothing. What are you doing?" replied Jimmy.

David would almost always respond, "Not much. Do you want to ask your parents if we can get together and hang out?"

Jimmy would put his hand over the mouthpiece of the phone and yell to his mom, "Can I go to David's house?"

"Sure, sweetie. Just make sure to be back before your dad gets home from work so we can have dinner together," she replied. Jimmy didn't like it when his mom called him "sweetie," especially since he was thirteen! This is why he covered the mouthpiece—he didn't want David to hear her and make fun of him. Jimmy put his mouth back to the phone, "She said I can play. I'll come right over!"

One evening David came over to Jimmy's house, and they got themselves in a bit of trouble. Jimmy had an older sister named Sarah. She was seventeen, and that night happened to be her senior prom. This prom night was all Jimmy had heard about for the last two months. Jimmy and Sarah didn't talk much, but they were pretty close for a brother and sister. Sarah had told Jimmy that this was to be the most important day of her senior year. Every few days Jimmy watched Sarah and their mom go shopping for "the dress," along with all of the essential "accessories," as they called them. He thought it was all pretty funny and a big waste of time.

Sarah's boyfriend, Todd, was taking her to the prom. Jimmy didn't like Todd too much. He treated Jimmy like a little kid and never paid much attention to him. Besides, before Todd came around, Jimmy and Sarah used to spend quite a bit of time together. With Todd in the picture, Sarah not only spent a lot of time with Todd instead of Jimmy, but she would NOT stop talking about how cute he was and how good he was at sports and stuff. All of that talk made Jimmy sick.

David knew that Jimmy didn't like Todd very much, and he came up with a master plan for prom night. When Todd came over to pick up Sarah and take pictures with the parents, David and Jimmy went to work. They said hello to Todd and acted as though they were excited for Sarah, Todd, and their prom night. But after making their friendly appearance, they went into the garage and out the door that led into the backyard, bringing with them a brown paper lunch bag. Jimmy had a dog named Ralphie who'd always go potty in the same spot. The boys ran over to the "dump zone," as they called it, and put a bunch of dog poo in the bag. After David made sure Todd and Sarah were still taking pictures, Jimmy ran out to Todd's car, squeezed his skinny arm through the slightly open car window, and unlocked the door. He then stuffed the bag full of poo under Todd's seat, quietly closed the door, and ran back to the safety of the garage. When Jimmy made it back, he and David couldn't control their laughter. They grabbed some towels out of the clothes dryer to put over their mouths so the rest of the family wouldn't hear them.

About ten minutes later, Sarah and Todd got into his car and drove off. But from the moment they got in, they both smelled something horrible—and neither one wanted to admit to noticing the odor in case the other one was having a bad case of gas or something. It was brutally awkward. They rode in silence as the smell became overwhelming. Their ride to dinner was going to take about forty-five minutes, and Todd could no longer handle the stench.

With a sheepish and embarrassed look on his face, he finally looked over at Sarah and said, "I smell something horrible, and I know it didn't come from me." As soon as Todd let the words out of his mouth, he knew he didn't phrase it right.

Sarah, with a horrified look on her face, replied, "Are you trying to say that disgusting smell is coming from me?!"

Todd quickly said, "No! Of course not! I just didn't want you to think it was coming from me!"

Sarah began to cry and then she yelled, "Turn the car around and take me home!"

When Todd's car came screeching into the driveway, Jimmy and David looked out Jimmy's bedroom window and began laughing hysterically. This time it wasn't a carefree laugh but a nervous laugh as they pictured what might happen when Todd and Sarah found out that they'd planted a bag of poo under the seat. They watched Sarah run out of the car and into the house while Todd frantically searched the car for whatever could be causing that smell. Moments later Todd ran up to the house and found Sarah crying in her mother's arms. He explained what he'd found, and about a minute later Sarah was pounding on Jimmy's door. It would be a week before Jimmy was allowed to "hang out" with David again.

This was the life of Jimmy and David. They were best buddies with endless stories like this prom-night incident. They were connected, and they didn't think life could get much better.

Despite their antics, Jimmy and David's parents gave them a little more freedom since they were now thirteen. When they weren't playing video games, they rode their mountain bikes down the street to a local shopping center. During the school year, they'd ride there after school a couple days a week. But during the summer, they'd ride their bikes there every day. They first started going because their parents told them to get some fresh air and rest their eyes from all the video games they played. Jimmy and David weren't happy about it at first, but then they found out the local pizza place had a video game arcade. It was AMAZING! It had all the newest games and most of them were two-player games, so they could fine-tune all of their military strategies and football formations. Playing these games took money away from their "home" video-game fund that they usually pooled their allowance money into. But they figured it was worth it.

Every day when they rode their bikes down the street, they saw this homeless-looking guy who pushed around an old shopping cart. He was really dirty, and he had bags full of empty aluminum cans in his cart. Sometimes he'd just be sitting under a tree to get out of the warm sun. Wherever he was or whatever he was doing, Jimmy and David made fun of him. As they rode their bikes past him, they'd throw dirt clods at him and yell out, "You dirty bum!" or "Why don't you go get a job!" They'd laugh and just keep riding by on their way to the video arcade. Jimmy and David named him "Recycle Can Guy," and they never thought about him other than the times when they had the chance to make fun of him or throw stuff at him.

Life for Jimmy and David was all about . . . Jimmy and David. Their goal in life was to have as much fun and make as much money as possible so they could buy more video games, eat a ton of candy, and watch lots of movies. Often they'd get all their buddies together and play video games all night long. Once they saw the sun coming up, they'd finally fall asleep and not wake up until the middle of the day. Then they'd play more video games or ride their bikes down to the shopping center, past Recycle Can Guy, and play some more video games at the arcade.

They weren't "bad" boys who did horrible things, but all their energy revolved around themselves. David and Jimmy couldn't see another way of living outside of the seriously limited perspective they had.

## Part II: Grandma's Death

Soon after the boys turned sixteen, Jimmy's grandmother became very ill. Jimmy wasn't really sure what she was sick with, but he did know that his mom spent a lot of time with his grandma. Often Jimmy's mom would encourage him to ride his bike over to his grandma's house to spend time with her and help her around her house. She lived only a few blocks away, so it wouldn't have been hard to do. But because Jimmy and David had lots of friends and always had things going on, Jimmy never made it a point to spend time with his grandma. *Besides*, he thought, *It's not like she's going to die!*

Every time Jimmy's mom asked him to go to his grandma's house with her, he'd come up with some excuse. Sometimes it was because he couldn't miss his flag football game. Other times it was because he and his buddies had been planning an all-night video game party that he just couldn't miss. Jimmy continued to live his "Jimmy-centered" life.

One day both of Jimmy's parents and his older sister, Sarah, decided to go spend some time with his grandma as her sickness worsened. They came into Jimmy's room to see if he'd go with them, and once again he came up with a clever excuse to avoid this distraction from his normal way of life. His family was disappointed that he wouldn't come, but they went over to Grandma's anyway.

Their time with Grandma that night was beautiful. It was filled with conversations about memories and sharing about hopes for the future. They were able to express how much they loved each other and gave lots of hugs. Jimmy missed it all.

As Jimmy's parents and sister interacted with Grandma that day, they could sense that it might be their last time with her. Her spirits were up, but her body was failing. It had been a slow and painful fight for her over the last few months. And late that evening, as they'd suspected, she died.

Jimmy got the news the next morning that Grandma had died. When he heard about her death, he was surprisingly unaffected. He was disappointed he wouldn't see her again, but he found many ways to convince himself that it wasn't that big a deal. *She lived a long life. She was bound to die sometime,* he'd think to himself. The next couple of days passed, and Jimmy continued to feel little remorse about his grandma's death and the fact that he didn't spend any time with her in her last days. This continued to be the case for Jimmy until one afternoon when his mom came into his room while he and David were playing video games. She asked Jimmy to come talk with her for a minute.

## Follow-Up Questions
- Can you identify with the lifestyle of Jimmy and David?

- Are there people in your life who you make fun of, walk by, or just ignore, rather than considering how you can help them? Who are these people?

- Is life as a human being—and more specifically, as a Christ-follower—only about having fun? What would a healthy life look like?

- Do you spend more time avoiding doing bad things than doing good things?

- Has there been a time that you've neglected someone (like Jimmy did) that you now regret?

## Part III: Painful Reflection

Jimmy could tell from the moment she walked into his room that his mom had something serious to share with him. They walked out to the living room and sat on the couch. He looked at her somber face and could tell she had a heavy heart. He asked, "What is it, Mom? What did you need to talk about?"

She looked back at Jimmy and explained that his grandmother really, really loved him. Jimmy's mom continued, "In fact, as her illness progressed, she would think about you more and more. But because she rarely got to see you in person to tell you how much she loved you, she wrote you this letter."

Jimmy took the letter from his mom's outstretched hand. His mother left the room, and he sat back into the couch and began to read.

Dear Jimmy,

I hope this letter finds you well, my loving grandson. From the day you were born 16 years ago, I have been proud to call myself your grandma. I can remember the first time you said my name, and at that point I looked forward to loving you as you grew to manhood.

There were times that I came over to your house for the week, and we'd get out of bed at midnight and play board games without telling your mom and dad . . . Sometimes we also snuck an ice cream bar out of the freezer and ate it before dinner. I remember reading stories to you at bedtime and taking you on walks along the creek while you skipped rocks. I can't think of any grandma who could be more proud of her grandson than I am of you, Jimmy.

As you grew older, I wish we could have spent more time together, but I knew you were busy with very important things. I would ask your mother what you were involved in and who you were spending your time with. As she talked about you, I couldn't help but smile as I pictured you living a full life that was leading to manhood.

Jimmy, I know my time is short. I want you to know that as I lie here in bed, I think of you and pray for you. In fact, I've prayed for you every day since you were born. I knew I wouldn't be able to physically be with you every day as you grew up, but I knew that I could simply pray for you. [At this point Jimmy thought of how rarely he ever thought about his grandma, let alone prayed for her.]

Finally, my grandson, I want to encourage you in one thing that I believe is the most important of anything I've ever told you. Jimmy, for so long my prayer for you has been that you'd explore the teachings and ways of Jesus and have a relationship with him. As I lie in bed, I often feel lonely and forgotten. There were many times that the peace I had through knowing Jesus was all I had to sustain me. Jimmy, EVERY person needs to be loved in some way, but some people don't have anyone to offer that to them. Others will see Jesus through your actions of service and love. Please don't ever get so caught up in your own responsibilities that you forget those who need to see Jesus **through** you the most.

I am very proud of you and love you very much, Jimmy. You are going to be—and are already—an amazing man.

*Your loving grandma*

When Jimmy finished reading the letter, it was as if his whole body went numb. He blankly stared at his grandma's letter. His numbness was soon followed by a surge of painful emotion. He began to lose it. Jimmy finally began to confront and question the life he'd been living so comfortably. He broke down in tears and went into a deep reflection of how little "service and love" he'd shown to those around him. Especially to his grandma—and even when she needed his service and love the most.

## Part IV: Exploring a New Kingdom

The next day David gave Jimmy his usual call to see if he wanted to get together and play some video games or ride bikes down to the shopping center. Jimmy loved David as his best friend, but hearing David's request to do the very thing that kept him from spending time with his grandma made Jimmy feel sick. He tried to hide most of his emotion when he responded to David by saying, "I think I'm going to just stay home today, but thanks for asking." David didn't think much of it and went off with the rest of their buddies for their usual activities.

Over the course of the next week, Jimmy withdrew from his friends, and especially from David. He'd stay at home and couldn't stop thinking about his grandma's request for him to do his best to love and serve as Jesus did. Jimmy wanted to know what that meant and why she seemed so passionate about his knowing Jesus. Jimmy believed that Jesus was the Son of God; in fact he often was the one who knew the most answers in the Sunday school classes he attended every week at church. But he never really thought about God, Jesus, or the Bible after he and his family left the church service. What did that have to do with his life here and now? Wasn't that just a bunch of "Christian" stories that no longer related to him today? Besides, he'd asked Jesus to come into his heart already—so his job was all done, right?

Still, Jimmy wanted to know more.

He remembered one of his Sunday school teachers had mentioned that the book of John said a lot about the life of this guy, Jesus. So he started studying every page. The more he read about Jesus, the more he was blown away by how radical his life and teachings were. Jimmy had a picture of Jesus being a soft-looking guy with a halo and a white tunic. Every once in a while, he pictured Jesus petting pure white sheep before floating into the clouds. This wasn't the Jesus he was discovering in his study of John. This Jesus said he brought about a kingdom that looked after the poor and the orphans and the widows. In this kingdom Jesus called his followers to love their enemies, turn the other cheek, and walk the extra mile. This kingdom wasn't designed to serve the religious or political elite, but bring hope to the broken, hurting, and lonely. Jesus prayed, "Your kingdom come, your will be done on earth as it is in heaven" (Matthew 6:10).

Jimmy couldn't get enough! He flipped forward a few books and ran into Philippians. He remembered a little bit about this guy Paul who wrote the letter, but he was curious about what he had to say. Jimmy read Philippians 2:1–4 NIV:

> If you have any encouragement from being united with Christ, if any comfort from his love, if any fellowship with the Spirit, if any tenderness and compassion, then make my joy complete by being like-minded, having the same love, being one in spirit and purpose. Do nothing out of selfish ambition or vain conceit, but in humility consider others better than yourselves. Each of you should look not only to your own interests, but also to the interests of others.

Jimmy's excitement and curiosity was now coupled with conviction and reflection on the life he was living. He looked back at Philippians 2:4, "Each of you should look not only to your own interests, but also to the interests of others." Jimmy again realized that he rarely considered anyone's interests except his own. If this was the life that Jesus wanted his people to live, then Jimmy hadn't been living it.

## Part V: A New Kind of Friendship

The next week, David began to get worried about his best buddy Jimmy, so he went over to his house to see how he was doing. As soon as Jimmy opened the front door after hearing David's knocks (he usually just walked in, but the door was locked), David could tell his friend wasn't the person he knew so well. There was something different about him. He didn't look different, but something was definitely strange.

David assumed this had something to do with Jimmy's grandma's death: "You seem down. I thought you weren't that close with your grandma."

Jimmy quickly responded while at the same time getting choked up: "That's exactly it! I failed to love and serve my grandma when she needed me most!" David could tell he was serious. They'd been best friends, but they'd never come close to crying in front of each other. This was all new territory for David, and he didn't know what to say or do.

After a long awkward silence, David finally told Jimmy that he shouldn't feel so bad about not spending a lot of time with his grandma. He continued, "You were busy with a lot of things, Jimmy. Don't be so hard on yourself."

Jimmy was again quick to respond, "I wasn't busy with things that mattered to anyone but me!" He grabbed the letter that his grandma had written to him, handed it to David, and said, "Read this."

David sat down on the same couch that Jimmy had sat in when he first read the letter, and he began to read. Jimmy watched David closely as his eyes worked through the letter. Jimmy could see that David was taking this seriously and was curious to know how he'd respond.

As David finished the letter, he looked up at Jimmy with a solemn feel. He didn't know what to say, so he gave Jimmy a hug, handed him the letter while saying goodbye, and walked out the door he'd just entered a few minutes earlier.

## Follow-Up Questions
- Can you relate to the pain and realization Jimmy comes to after reading his grandma's letter?
- Have you ever slowed down long enough to ask yourself, "Do I love and serve others in the way Jesus did?"
- What was it that kept you from living this kind of life?
- How do you respond to Philippians 2:1–4, which tells us to take on the interests of others, not just our own?
- Jimmy yelled, "I wasn't busy with things that mattered to anyone but me!" How do you respond to that statement?

## Part VI: New Eyes—Participating in the Kingdom of God

Over the course of the next week, Jimmy began to hang out with his friends once again. But this time he viewed their actions and activities with new eyes. He was no longer content with how they'd been living for so long. When his buddies spent all their money on one video game or made fun of homeless men or women as they passed them, Jimmy didn't feel as though he could participate with them in good conscience. There had to be a different way of doing things. A way that wasn't so empty and meaningless.

Toward the end of the week, David came over to Jimmy's house after school. It was just the two of them, and as they instinctively started to walk back to Jimmy's room to play video games, David said, "I have something I need to talk to you about, Jimmy."

Jimmy, with a bit of a confused look on his face, sat on the couch in the living room and asked, "What's going on?" David wasn't sure how to say it, but he admitted he'd really been thinking about Jimmy's grandma's letter since he'd read it. Jimmy's best buddy went on to explain that he felt his life had also been only focused on himself, and he wanted to do something about it. This news thrilled Jimmy! He was not alone!

David continued, "I do have to ask you a question though, Jimmy. Do you just want to change because you feel guilty about ignoring your grandma?"

Jimmy calmly responded, "I do regret what I DIDN'T do. But I truly believe I need and want to do better at living as Jesus did—especially how he loved and served others."

With that, David explained that he'd be willing to begin studying Jesus' life and experiment with Jimmy in what it looks like to live more in tune with Jesus and his ways.

## Part VII: The Life of a Revolutionary

Jimmy guided David to the book of John where he'd recently discovered how incredibly radical this guy Jesus was. They studied his life and then flipped back to the book of Matthew and studied the long invitation to a new way of living that Jesus gave his followers, called the Sermon on the Mount:

> ³ *Blessed are the poor in spirit, for theirs is the kingdom of heaven.*
>
> ⁴ *Blessed are those who mourn, for they will be comforted.*
>
> ⁵ *Blessed are the meek, for they will inherit the earth.*
>
> ⁶ *Blessed are those who hunger and thirst for righteousness, for they will be filled.*

*⁷ Blessed are the merciful, for they will be shown mercy.*

*⁸ Blessed are the pure in heart, for they will see God.*

*⁹ Blessed are the peacemakers, for they will be called sons of God.*

*¹⁰ Blessed are those who are persecuted because of righteousness, for theirs is the kingdom of heaven.*

Matthew 5:3–10 NIV

Their minds could barely wrap around how different Jesus' message was compared to what they'd been taught all their lives. Jesus was a great speaker, and he always preached for the rights of the hurting, poor, and oppressed. But there was something glaringly clear about his life that really stood out to them: Jesus didn't just *talk* about loving and serving; he backed up everything he said with his actions. He healed the sick, hung out with the lonely, forgave sinners, and fed the hungry. This Jesus was a God of action.

Jimmy and David each came to the realization that if their faith was real, it was going to have to take the form of action—today, tomorrow, and every day. If they were going to truly believe in, trust in, and follow Jesus, then they'd have to put down their video games and serve Jesus through loving the hungry, the thirsty, the naked, the sick, and the lonely (Matthew 25:35–36). Their stories needed to merge with God's story by making a 180-degree turn into God's kingdom. The boys suddenly looked at each other and in a moment of conviction, excitement, and hope shouted, "Recycle Can Guy!"

## Part VIII: Partnering in the Mission of God

Even though both Jimmy and David had their driver's licenses, they still preferred riding down to the shopping center on their bikes. The boys ran to the garage, jumped on their bikes, and headed toward the shopping center and Recycle Can Guy. With each turn of their pedals, they were filled with anticipation over their first interaction with Recycle Can Guy that didn't involve rude comments or throwing things at him.

In a matter of minutes, they saw him a hundred yards ahead on the side of the road with his cart full of cans. As they got closer, they noticed that

Recycle Can Guy began to hide behind a nearby tree. When they pulled up to say hello, he wouldn't even look at them for fear that they'd hurl insults or throw rocks at him. But nothing they said made him come out of hiding. They were crushed. "How are we supposed to love and serve others like Jesus did when they won't even talk to us?" asked David.

Not discouraged by their first encounter with Recycle Can Guy, Jimmy and David rode their bikes down to see him every day after school for the next week. Friday afternoon started the same way. They jumped on their bikes and rode down to the man they hoped to befriend. Expecting to once again be ignored, something different happened this afternoon. As the boys came up to Recycle Can Guy, he didn't run away and hide. Instead, he stood his ground and looked them in the eyes as they walked toward him.

He asked, "Why do you boys keep coming down here?"

Jimmy, shocked that he was speaking to them, responded, "We want to apologize for how we've treated you for so many years. We were wrong. We just wanted to apologize and ask if you'd be willing to forgive us and maybe have a conversation some time." Recycle Can Guy didn't say much else that day, but it was the beginning of something beautiful.

With each passing day, Recycle Can Guy began to trust Jimmy and David more and more. In fact he came to realize they weren't trying to hurt him but trying to serve him. Each day the boys would hear a little bit more of Recycle Can Guy's story. He even told them his name was Henry. Now he was a real person to them—no longer just a poor guy on the side of the road.

A few days after Jimmy and David learned Henry's name, David brought up an idea: "You know how we always do our best to save up all of our money so we can buy the newest video games? What if we used some of that money to take Henry out to lunch tomorrow?"

Jimmy hesitated. Money wasn't easy to come by, and he'd never really thought about doing all of that work to save it up just so he could turn around and give it away! But as he thought more about it, he began to reflect on one point in Jesus' life when he challenged his followers to give all of their possessions to the poor and follow him. It was a scary thought, but Jimmy knew he hadn't come close to giving everything he had to the poor (Matthew 19:21; Mark 10:21). He looked back at David and said, "Let's do it!"

The boys jumped on their bikes and headed down to Henry's usual hangout spot. As they arrived they both were so excited to ask him to lunch that they blurted out, "Do you want to come eat some lunch with us?" Even though Henry had come to trust Jimmy and David to some degree, he was still a bit taken back by their offer. He couldn't remember the last time he'd been offered the opportunity to go to lunch inside a restaurant.

After some hesitation, Henry looked up at the two anxious boys and said, "I would like that."

Jimmy and David carried Henry's big bags full of cans that he'd collected that morning, and they walked their bikes alongside him on the way to their favorite local café. They walked in and took seats across the table from Henry so they both could look him in the eye as they talked. As the conversation began to unfold, Jimmy and David realized that the money they spent on this meal was far more fulfilling than any video game, skateboard, or bag of candy they'd purchased in the past.

They asked Henry to tell them his story. It was a story full of joy and sadness, wholeness and brokenness, and pleasure and pain. Their new friend shared that his wife had died twenty years earlier of breast cancer. She was the love of his life. They did everything together. From traveling across the world to sharing coffee every morning before leaving for work, she was his only love. They had only one child, as his wife was unable to have children after their daughter's difficult birth. He loved his daughter very much. In fact, when he began to share about her, he got choked up and could barely describe their relationship. The topic brought him great joy and terrible grief. Henry explained that his daughter withdrew from him completely once her mother passed away. He hadn't spoken to her in seven or eight years, but it was evident he loved her more than ever.

Henry went on to share that his wife's death and his daughter's withdrawal had led him to into a deep depression. The only "cure" he could find was through drug use. Drugs removed him from the reality and pain of life, if only for a short time. Within a year, he was addicted and lost the factory job he'd held for more than thirty years. Again, he was crushed. As a result, he took more and more drugs and couldn't find or keep any form of employment. The people he'd considered his closest friends completely abandoned him, as they considered him a lost cause. They wanted nothing to do with a depressed addict of a friend. Henry was all alone.

As Henry was telling his story, Jimmy and David sat across from him stunned and overwhelmed. They thought, *This is WAY bigger than any video game or movie night! What have we gotten ourselves into?* Although nervous and even a bit scared, they both had a peace like never before.

They'd begun to participate in the redemptive and restorative story of Jesus.

Henry continued sharing his life story with the boys. He told them that every day he regretted his decision to start doing drugs. He was VERY angry with himself, and it only led him to take more. Years earlier he'd entered a recovery program hoping to conquer his many addictions. He began to cry, "I wanted to get better, but I just felt like I was another number. It didn't seem as though anyone really cared about getting to know me and share life with me." As a result he again found himself alone and addicted. He felt that no one really cared if he got better, so he just gave up and led a life of trying to get as much money as possible to feed his drug addictions. If he had any extra money, he'd buy himself some food. Henry was now a broken, skinny, depressed, and very lonely man. He was seventy-one years old and saw no hope for change.

Jimmy and David, shocked by what they'd just heard, scrambled for any response. Then Jimmy finally blurted, "So where do you live?" Henry explained that he lived in a small storage closet right next to the janitor closet underneath a nearby apartment complex. He said the manager was very nice. And as long as Henry didn't tell too many people about where he was staying, the manager let him sleep there. The boys asked if he'd let them come over and help him clean or bring him some groceries sometime. Henry was really embarrassed at their offer. He knew how unbearably dirty, dark, and smelly his room was, and it made him even more depressed picturing two sixteen-year-old boys helping him out. Jimmy and David's friend declined their offer, but they decided they weren't going to stop asking him in the following weeks.

Over the next week and a half, Jimmy and David continued to offer their services of cleaning and bringing some food over to Henry's room. Although very hesitant, he finally accepted their offer, and all three of them headed to Henry's.

Jimmy and David expected it to be a disturbing setting, but as they walked down the narrow, dark staircase, it was far worse than they'd imagined. There was concrete everywhere, most of the lights didn't work, and it smelled of a combination of gas, garbage, and urine. They passed the janitor's closet that was full of dirty mops and chemical cleaners and turned into Henry's room. It was a mess. There were no signs of life or hope. They couldn't help but feel a bit depressed in this setting. Although they were both overwhelmed, they didn't let Henry catch on to their true reactions. Both Jimmy and David continued talking with him as they entered the room and tried to break any awkwardness that Henry may have been feeling due to the embarrassing state of his home.

This small room became the focus of Jimmy and David's lives over the next week. To them it wasn't just a dirty, small room. It was an opportunity to live out the Way of Jesus. It became their symbol of hope, restoration, and redemption—as this little room is made right, perhaps their good friend Henry would see Christ in its transformation, as well as in the service of Jimmy and David. They were determined to show Henry that he was very loved. Not only by them, but also by God. His life did have meaning, and he wasn't alone. Over the next week, the boys cleaned, organized, and repaired this small space every day after school. And the whole time Henry was watching their lives—closely.

## Part IX: Repenting (Turning) to a Life Lived in the Kingdom of God

One afternoon later that week, the boys made their usual trip to Henry's room to continue cleaning and talking. On the way over there, they picked up a few sandwiches at a local café. When they walked into Henry's place, they ate with him.

And as they ate, their new friend asked them a question. "Why are you boys doing all of this for some old drug addict you met on the side of the street?" Jimmy and David looked at each other; they both knew why they did these things, but they were unsure how to explain it. Jimmy quickly remembered an amazing story in the book of John that he'd recently read. It was a story that felt a lot like this, so he pulled out his Bible and began to read:

> *¹ But Jesus went to the Mount of Olives.*

> *² At dawn he appeared again in the temple courts, where all the people gathered around him, and he sat down to teach them.*

> *³ The teachers of the law and the Pharisees brought in a woman caught in adultery. They made her stand before the group*

> *⁴ and said to Jesus, "Teacher, this woman was caught in the act of adultery.*

*⁵ In the Law Moses commanded us to stone such women. Now what do you say?"*

*⁶ They were using this question as a trap, in order to have a basis for accusing him. But Jesus bent down and started to write on the ground with his finger.*

*⁷ When they kept on questioning him, he straightened up and said to them, "If any one of you is without sin, let him be the first to throw a stone at her."*

*⁸ Again he stooped down and wrote on the ground.*

*⁹ At this, those who heard began to go away one at a time, the older ones first, until only Jesus was left, with the woman still standing there.*

*¹⁰ Jesus straightened up and asked her, "Woman, where are they? Has no one condemned you?"*

*¹¹ "No one, sir," she said. "Then neither do I condemn you," Jesus declared. "Go now and leave your life of sin."*

John 8:1–11 NIV

Jimmy, still quite unsure of himself when it came to explaining his faith with words, went on to say, "I'm a lot like that woman. I've sinned over and over again in my life for as long as I can remember. My life was all about me. In fact, my grandma recently died, and I didn't even make an effort to spend time with her in her last days." Jimmy began to get a bit choked up, but continued, "Jesus could have 'stoned' me like those dudes wanted to do to that woman in the story, but he forgave me instead. He forgave me just like he forgave the woman; he asked me to leave my life of sin and participate in his kingdom. So I did. I've read a lot about Jesus lately, and I've seen that there's a new kingdom that he calls each of us to live in every day. It's a kingdom of love, and I think I should do my best to show that love to as many people as possible. That's why we do all this for you."

Henry was amazed and confused all at the same time. He said, "So would you guys consider yourselves Christians?" David replied, "Yes, we do." Henry continued, "I've met a lot of people who say they're Christians, but I've never met anyone who actually lived like this guy Jesus." He was intrigued.

## Part X: Growing Closer to Henry

About a week later, Jimmy and David jumped on their bikes to head over to Henry's for their daily visit. It was a cold and rainy day, so they made sure to wear raincoats and ride their bikes as fast as possible. They pulled into the parking lot outside of Henry's room and walked down the cement steps toward his modest—but now very clean and hope-filled—room. When they turned the corner and looked into his room, they noticed he wasn't there. A bit confused and a little bit concerned, Jimmy and David jumped back on their bikes and pedaled as fast as they could to the spot where they used to see Henry collecting cans.

As they pulled off to the side of the road and stepped off their bikes again, they still didn't see Henry. They called out his name as they searched behind the low-hanging trees and thick bushes. But Henry was nowhere to be found. Now feeling much more concerned about their friend, Jimmy and David got back on their bikes and headed to the local shopping center where they'd spent so much time over the years.

The boys rode all around the shopping center looking for Henry. Finally, they spotted him huddled over a small cup of coffee and sitting on the sidewalk right outside the café where they'd taken him weeks before. With great relief, they jumped off their bikes and took a seat on each side of him. Jimmy was the first to speak, "So Henry, how are you doing today? We've been looking for you everywhere!"

As soon as Henry looked up, both boys could see that he had rivers of tears streaming down his face. "I'm not doing very well today, boys," Henry responded. Jimmy and David froze and weren't exactly sure what to say, so they said nothing. Henry jumped back in, "I wasn't planning on telling you guys, because I didn't want to be a bother. But since we've become such close friends over the last couple of months, I can't imagine keeping this to myself."

David quietly said, "What is it, Henry? We want to help you out with whatever it is."

Henry began, "It was three years ago. My chest hurt really badly. Every time I'd take a breath, I would freeze up in pain." He continued, "I was able to get in and see a doctor, and he told me I had the early stages of lung cancer and I'd have only a few years to live." Tears were again streaming down Henry's face and now even the boys were getting choked up. "I think I'm in my last days, fellas," said Henry.

As had happened numerous times in their relationship with Henry, David and Jimmy were blown away by the power of the situation they'd chosen to be a part of. More than ever they knew this was WAY bigger than any video game or sleepover. This was real life, and there weren't any fantasylands for them to escape to. While they both struggled with these realizations, they each knew this was the life they should've been living from the moment they were born. They'd merged their stories with God's story, and now they found themselves right in the center of something way bigger than themselves.

They boys helped Henry back to his room underneath the apartment complex, gave him some food, and headed back home. Jimmy and David's parents knew about their interactions with Henry. Neither were thrilled about it and felt a bit uncomfortable, but they didn't stop the boys from befriending him. So when the boys got back home that evening, they told their parents Henry's WHOLE story and asked if they'd be willing to help them take care of him as his sickness got worse. After hearing everything their boys shared, both David's and Jimmy's parents said they'd love to do whatever they could to bring hope to this man Henry whom their boys couldn't stop talking about.

## Part XI: Living Loudly

Over the next three weeks, Jimmy and David made it their mission to love and serve Henry in the same way that Jesus had and continued to love and serve them. Henry's sickness had progressed, and he could no longer leave his room. Every day Jimmy and David, along with their families and even some friends, would go to Henry's room to bring food, warm things to drink, and healthy conversation. Each person who got involved couldn't help but sense love and compassion like they'd never experienced before. Participating with God in this way was powerful. It was doing something to each of them, and they'd never be the same.

Toward the end of the three weeks, Jimmy and David went over by themselves to bring some dinner to Henry. They ate, laughed, and had a great time together. Near the end of the evening, Henry looked up at both boys as tears filled his eyes. He said, "I haven't felt love like this since my wife died 20 years ago." Henry began to sob now. It wasn't a sad sob; it was a sob full of joy and peace. He continued, "I remember what you guys said about Jesus. If that Jesus loves me half as much as you boys have loved me, then I want to know him the way you do."

Jimmy, filled with excitement, hope, and joy like he'd never before experienced, responded, "He doesn't love you as much as we've loved you; he loves you much more."

That was the last time Jimmy and David ever talked to Henry—he passed away later that evening.

## Part XII: The Story Continues

Jimmy and David still love to think back to their times with their good friend, Henry. They're thirty years old now and can still recall every detail of their story together—not because of what they'd done for Henry, but because of what Henry had done for them. Their time with Henry allowed them, for the first time in their lives, to turn from living only for themselves to living in partnership with God and his mission of redemption and restoration. They now see themselves as partners in bringing God's kingdom to earth. It was a story they could be a part of today, tomorrow, and every day forward.

Jesus once said, "Repent [or turn]: for the kingdom of heaven is at hand" (Matthew 4:17 KJV). Jimmy and David had repented. Their lives had turned 180 degrees. Their story met God's story, and they realized that was the way it was supposed to be all along.

### Follow-Up Questions

- Have you ever been like David and watched a friend go through a situation that led to him or her changing for the better?

- Do you find it scary to walk up to people you don't know and start talking to them? More specifically, how about talking to homeless people?

- What are some other types of people we may be called to serve who aren't such extreme cases?

- Would you be willing to spend the money you normally spend on yourself for the good of someone else? Can you relate to Jimmy and David when they said that spending money on Henry was way better than buying any video game?

- Do you have friends with whom you can experiment in living radically in the Way of Jesus?

- What's more effective: Telling others about Jesus or *showing* them Jesus through your actions? Why is that?

# 10

# CHLOE

## Topics—Depression, Loneliness, False Identity, Cutting, Spiritual Bulimia

Chloe was a middle child. She had an older brother named Jake and a younger sister named Katie. For as long as she could remember, Chloe had felt like the outcast, the third best, the forgotten child. While she was great at softball and did well in school, her family never seemed to acknowledge her accomplishments as worthwhile. It was always about Jake and Katie.

When the family went on vacation, all three kids would have to sit in the backseat of the car. Of course, Chloe would get stuck in the middle of the bench seat. This meant that while Jake and Katie were sound asleep with their heads resting comfortably against the windows, Chloe was constantly snapped out of her dreams whenever her neck fell forward, left, or right. Even when they were all awake, she felt isolated from the conversation. Jake and Katie didn't usually get along with each other; but when Chloe sat between them, they seemed to have a bunch of inside jokes that they'd pass back and forth while Chloe tried to lean away from their banter.

By the time she was thirteen, Chloe had grown accustomed to these dynamics and didn't know any other way to view "family." This was the hand she'd been dealt, and she figured other people must have it worse than she did. That is, she believed that was true until one afternoon when she overheard her brother talking with one of his buddies. The two guys didn't know Chloe was standing around the corner when Jake told his friend, "I don't know what it is, but I just don't like Chloe as much as I do Katie. Chloe is kinda weird, and she isn't any fun to be around." Chloe was crushed, but she walked by the boys without letting on that she'd heard what Jake had said.

Because Chloe didn't have friendships with her brother or sister and often felt forgotten by her parents, she made it her mission to have as many friends as possible. She spent countless hours on social networking sites seeking out virtual friends. Every time she saw her "friend" count increase to a number that was bigger than her brother's, sister's, or other friends', she'd feel a rush of accomplishment and security. She wanted to be known, and she became willing to do anything to bring as much positive attention to herself as possible. But the longer Chloe lived this virtual life, the more insecure she became in her God-given identity.

Throughout junior high and into her first couple years of high school, Chloe never missed a youth group event at her family's church. She was the first to raise her hand with the "right" answer in Sunday school, and everyone came to know her as the perfect "Christian" kid. Adults complimented her parents on raising such an outgoing, smart, godly child. Chloe said all the right things, did all the right things, and had everyone fooled . . . even herself. Everything seemed to be working out perfectly—until one of her youth group leaders asked Chloe to have an honest conversation with her.

*(Good place to stop for the week and have conversation.)*

The leader's name was Debbie, and Chloe felt like Debbie often had a watchful eye on her and didn't "buy" Chloe's act. After three years of making as many friends as humanly possible, gaining the respect of all the adults at her church, and continuing to do well in school, even Chloe thought she'd found her true identity. But Debbie suspected that was far from the truth.

After youth group one night, Chloe was talking in a circle of her girlfriends when she felt a tap on her shoulder. She turned and saw Debbie standing there. From the moment she looked into Debbie's eyes, something in her stomach didn't feel right. Debbie asked if they could talk for a few minutes, so they walked to a nearby bench and sat down. In her three years of "acting," Chloe had never been asked to have an honest, one-on-one conversation. So she felt very uncomfortable. Debbie asked a few simple questions, which Chloe quickly answered with her usual fake smile.

After a few moments of silence, Debbie asked, "Have you always had so many friends and been so outgoing?" All of Chloe's painful, lonely experiences flashed through her memory in the blink of an eye. She tried to shake off her discomfort with a faint smile and shallow response, but she couldn't pull it off. At that moment, though, Chloe saw her dad pull into the parking lot to pick her up. Without making eye contact with Debbie, she said goodbye and quickly walked to the apparent safety of her father's car.

When Chloe got home, she walked straight to her room and began crying hysterically. She wasn't even sure *why* she was crying, but she couldn't help herself. Through her tears she started to realize that she'd become a hollow, fake shell, and no one really knew who she was. She didn't even know who she was anymore. At this she felt more alone and depressed than ever.

The next day at school, Chloe kept smiling and remained the center of attention among her friends. But inside she was broken and hurting. Over the past year Chloe had heard some of her friends talking about "cutting." She wasn't sure what it meant, but for some reason she felt drawn to try it. After school she locked her bedroom door and began sobbing again at the empty reality of her life. In between the tears, she began cutting her forearms with a knife she'd taken from the kitchen. At first she was scared, but she soon felt a kind of relief. There was something about this physical pain that lessened the pain in her soul. It became a release from her emotional pain.

Over the course of the next few weeks, Chloe would wake up each day and go back into her world while acting as if everything was fine. She didn't dare reveal her pain to anyone, as she feared it would ruin her perfect reputation. She felt as though her loneliness and depression was a battle she had to fight alone. This led her down a destructive path, and Chloe became addicted to cutting—her only release from all of the emotional baggage she was carrying. Her parents were more comfortable with the image she'd established over the last three years, so they didn't ask her any questions; and since Chloe had never experienced a true friendship, she knew of no other alternatives than taking it on alone. She continued to attend every possible church function on a weekly basis, where she'd also see Debbie. But Chloe quickly avoided engaging in any conversation with her.

During the message at youth group one evening, Chloe became overwhelmed with emotion and left the room as though she needed to use the restroom. Instead, she ran out to the parking lot, sat on the curb, and started sobbing into her hands. About two minutes later, she felt a hand on her back and was startled. When Chloe looked up, she saw Debbie sitting next to her, and her eyes were full of tears as well. For the next fifteen minutes, Debbie simply held Chloe, and they both cried like never before. For some reason, this felt real to Chloe. It was as if she was experiencing her true identity for the first time, but she had no idea how to deal with it.

The next week, Chloe approached Debbie and asked if they could talk. For once Chloe didn't want the "right" Christian answers that she'd always spouted without thinking. And Debbie didn't give them to her. She simply told Chloe that healing was possible, but she needed to be vulnerable and could no longer hold stuff in or deal with it on her own. All Chloe heard was the terrifying word *vulnerable*, and she knew it would mean losing her reputation, friendships, and fake identity. This sounded really scary, and it turned Chloe off from anything else Debbie said.

*(Good place to stop for the week and have conversation.)*

A few nights later Chloe was again cutting her arms in her bedroom. But she cut too much and lost so much blood that she blacked out. Her mom called her name to let her know that dinner was ready, but there was no response. Because Chloe's parents knew nothing of the pain she was going through, her mom wasn't concerned; but she went to Chloe's room to check on her anyway. She found Chloe lying on her bed, blacked out, and surrounded by blood. Chloe's parents rushed her to the hospital, and the doctors were able to stabilize her.

About twenty-four hours later, although extremely groggy and with blurred vision, Chloe woke up. Her first conscious thought was not relief but disappointment. This experience had impacted her so much that she wished she'd just died. As she began to move her head, she saw a figure sitting next to her. Trying hard to focus, Chloe felt a hand on her arm. The touch felt familiar. As her eyes focused enough for her to see more clearly, she saw that the figure was her youth leader, Debbie. At first Chloe felt nervous because Debbie had come to represent vulnerability and truth. But then she quickly remembered the feeling of crying in Debbie's arms and how real she felt in her soul in that moment.

Again, Debbie just held Chloe and didn't give her any answers. She simply told Chloe how much she was worth and how much she personally cared about her. Like water bursting from a pipe that had been stuffed closed for years with leaves and dirt, Chloe began pouring out her past hurt, pain, and fears to Debbie. And Debbie just listened.

After some processing, Debbie began to understand that Chloe was depressed because of her past loneliness and isolation in her family. Chloe had put on a "show" and became what Debbie called "spiritually bulimic." Chloe had "eaten" a great deal of "church stuff," but none of it had actually been digested. So Chloe had just vomited it back out in the form of "right" answers and actions and kept on going. She hadn't experienced a spirituality of wholeness; it was a counterfeit image. Chloe hadn't had the opportunity to seek out a faith of her own by asking authentic questions and having real experiences because she'd been fed the right answers and quickly reproduced them. Debbie believed that spiritual bulimics could fall victim to missing out on the powerful, transforming mystery of the Bible and our call to be part of that Story, as the bulimia caused a redundant, numb view of Scripture.

Chloe decided she wanted to kick her spiritual bulimia and seek healing from the pain that her false identity had caused her so she could enter more fully into her identity as a follower of Jesus. She wanted her faith to be her own—not her parents', her friends', or her youth leader's. Chloe also knew that cutting was no longer an option as a release from her emotional pain. Instead, she wanted to find people who'd support her in breaking this addiction. Although being vulnerable was the scariest reality for Chloe, she knew it truly is the most real.

## Follow-Up Questions

- What could you relate to in Chloe's story? Why?

- Have you ever felt as though you knew more than enough about the Bible or you've heard the same things so many times that they seemed boring or like they didn't relate to you? Why do you suppose that happens to those of us who've been part of a church for a long time?

- Have you ever tried to cover up issues in your life by being overly outgoing and giving all the "right" answers so no one would think something was wrong?

- Have you ever been surrounded by a ton of people or friends but still felt completely alone?

- Have you ever known anyone who's been involved with cutting? What do you think brings a person to that point? How did you respond when you found out? Do you think this person was trying to commit suicide or just looking for relief?

# 11

# KEVIN AND CHARLIE

*Topics—Redemptive Violence (and Its Conse-
quences), Injustice, Forgiveness, Reconciliation,
Restoration*

Once again Kevin found himself sitting across the desk from his school
principal. "Why do you get in so many fights?" asked the principal. "Is
there some reason you can't walk away when you get angry?" Kevin had
no response. He just sat low in the oversized chair and looked at the floor.
The principal continued, "If you don't have anything to say, then I don't
have any way to help you, Kevin. I'm going to have to call your parents and
suspend you for the next five days." Kevin accepted his fate, stormed out of
the office, and sat outside on the curb next to the campus supervisor, waiting for his parents to pick him up.

Kevin was a skinny nine-year-old kid who carried himself like he was
18, always watched his back, and had the temper of a viper. He was the kid
who either picked a fight or ended a fight by lashing out at someone if he
felt that person had wronged him.

He grew up in a pretty tough neighborhood, but his family life was even
tougher. Whether it was his father yelling at his mother or "disciplining"
Kevin and his younger sister, Tara, there always seemed to be some kind of
conflict at home. Kevin figured this was the way all families worked. Plus,
he didn't feel like he could blame his dad for his violent actions. His father
has been wounded during the Vietnam War and now walked with a perma-
nent limp. "If we could just blow up all of our enemies, this country could
finally be at peace!" his dad would say while watching the evening news.
Sometimes Kevin felt the same way about his "enemies" at school.

Whether Kevin was in a fight with a neighborhood bully or another kid
on the school playground, his dad always supported him: "Son, the most

important thing to do is to stand up for yourself. If you have to throw a punch or talk back to save face, then that's what you've gotta do." Kevin did what his father said, and he couldn't remember a single time he'd let someone get away with making fun of him or taking cheap shots at him.

This angry kid who retaliated in most every situation only became fiercer as he grew up through middle school and high school. Every faculty member knew him by his first name, and many of them had had to help break up his fights. Most of the faculty felt bad for him. He was so angry and confused, but he wasn't about to change his ways—and if he did, his parents would disown him. For Kevin, everything was "us" (his family, close friends, country) versus "them" (anyone outside of who he considered to be "us").

Kevin was eighteen years old when he heard a rumor going around the high school about his fifteen-year-old sister, Tara. Some of Kevin's friends had heard an eighteen-year-old boy named Cory calling Tara a whore and saying that she was having sex with a bunch of the older guys—including himself. Immediately Kevin was filled with rage and wanted to meet this guy in the parking lot after school. All of Kevin's friends knew about his temper and made sure he didn't do anything he'd regret that day.

Kevin couldn't sleep that night because he was filled with hatred and bitterness toward Cory. He thought, *This guy needs to pay for what he's done, and I'll make sure I'm the one who collects.* Kevin came up with a plan, and the next day he was going to put it into action.

Word passed through the school about a showdown between Kevin and Cory that afternoon in the parking lot. The whole school was buzzing, and Kevin enjoyed every minute of it. He didn't usually carry a gun, but his dad had given him one when he was fourteen—just in case he ever needed to use it in self-defense. As he dressed for school that morning, Kevin tucked the gun under his belt and against his lower back so his shirt covered it.

After the last bell rang, most of the students had boarded the school buses and headed home. But a few stayed back in the parking lot to see what would happen between Cory and Kevin. Each boy was standing by his own car when the two of them made eye contact and began walking toward each other. Kevin threw the first blow, and it sent Cory to the ground. Cory quickly jumped up and pushed Kevin into a retaining wall. Kevin fell shoulder-first onto the concrete. As he was getting up, Kevin saw one of the campus supervisors running toward them to stop the fight. Before he could get there, Kevin pulled out his gun and pointed it at Cory. Everyone stopped and stared in disbelief. Kevin felt as though his blood was pumping through his body at a blinding speed. This confused and angry boy began shaking, and his grip on the gun was loosening. Then suddenly he fired.

The next day, a well-dressed older fellow walked into Kevin's jail cell. Kevin hadn't said a word since the events of the day before. The man looked Kevin in the eye and said, "My name is Doug. I'll be representing you as your attorney. Cory died last night at the hospital. Since you turned eighteen last week, you'll be tried as an adult."

Kevin felt paralyzed by this news. What had happened to his life? How could he be facing a life sentence in prison? Was there something he was missing?

*(Good place to stop for the week and have conversation—see questions.)*

## Follow-Up Questions

- Why would a bad family life lead a person to act out in other parts of his or her life?

- What's our natural tendency when someone hurts us?

Someone had to be blamed for this situation. *How about Doug?* Kevin thought. *No, he did a good job representing me; it just didn't work out like he'd hoped. How about my sister? No, she never asked me to defend her, and I don't think she did sleep with all of those guys. Could it have been my fault? Not a chance. I only did what I needed to do. Plus, that's how I was taught to handle conflict growing up . . . growing up! That's it! My parents—they're the ones to blame. They knew something like this would happen to me, and they didn't say a thing! All of my life I saw only revenge, violence, and anger. This is all their fault.*

Kevin's bitterness toward his parents grew every day. As a result he isolated himself from everyone. This is what had become of him. He was serving a life sentence in prison, and he had no desire to communicate with anyone, not even his family.

That is, until Kevin met a guy named Charlie.

Charlie knew Kevin didn't want to talk, but after seeing Kevin sitting by himself at every meal for over a year, he sat down across the table from him anyway. Kevin didn't look up, so Charlie simply said hello and introduced himself. He already knew Kevin's name, so he didn't bother asking. In fact, Charlie didn't ask Kevin any questions; he just started telling his story.

Charlie had lived a simple life in a small mountain town. When he was twenty-one years old, he ran into an old friend who was back in town for the week visiting family and friends. Apparently his friend had some enemies because while they were eating dinner at a restaurant, someone started shouting at him to get out of town. Charlie wasn't sure what the story was. But he figured that if this guy wanted to yell, then they'd yell back. They started fighting; and after getting punched in the face, Charlie picked up a chair and slammed it over the guy's head. Somehow the chair hit the man's temple, and he died instantly. Now Charlie was in prison with a life sentence.

Although Kevin was still looking down and pretending to be interested in his dinner, he heard every word. Charlie continued, "I've learned a lot as a result of that night, Kevin. Maybe sometime we could talk more about it. And I'd be interested to hear your story as well." That was the first time anyone had paid any attention to Kevin.

The next afternoon Charlie came up to Kevin again while the inmates were outside in the courtyard. Kevin was sitting against a chain-link fence, and Charlie sat down right next to him. They didn't say much, but Kevin found himself appreciating the company. All of a sudden, Kevin started talking. He had no idea where it was coming from, but he just felt the need to tell his story. So he did. He discussed his childhood leading all the way up to the day he killed Cory. And he told Charlie about all of the bitterness he had toward his family, especially his parents. Kevin also shared about the guilt he carried around with him every day for murdering Cory.

It was like a small weight had been lifted off Kevin's shoulders. Even so, Kevin still remained hostile toward the other guys in the prison, and he began picking fights with anyone who seemed like an "enemy." It was as though he was transitioning from a quiet, isolated, and bitter person back into the angry, hostile person of his youth.

One day while they were back outside in the courtyard, Charlie pulled Kevin aside and began telling him another story—about this guy, Jesus, and his revolutionary way of dealing with people who disagreed with him or meant to harm him. Kevin had seen Bibles on TV before when those crazy preachers were on at 2 a.m. But when Charlie pulled his Bible from his pocket, it was the first time Kevin had seen one *in person*. Charlie opened his Bible to Matthew 5:38–42 and told Kevin that this was how Jesus taught his followers to respond to injustice:

> You have heard that it was said, "Eye for eye, and tooth for tooth." [39]But I tell you,
> Do not resist an evil person. If someone strikes you on the right cheek, turn to him

the other also. ⁴⁰And if someone wants to sue you and take your tunic, let him have your cloak as well. ⁴¹If someone forces you to go one mile, go with him two miles. ⁴²Give to the one who asks you, and do not turn away from the one who wants to borrow from you.

Charlie began to explain that when Jesus said these words, the Roman Empire ruled the land, and Israel was a small minority that was supposed to change the world as God's "chosen people." The Roman soldiers would often humiliate the Israelites as an act of lording their power over a submitted people. But in this passage Jesus suggests a creative third way of responding to the injustice that the Romans imposed on the less powerful.

Then Charlie said, "When I was growing up, I thought there were only two ways to respond to someone who tried to hurt me: I could either react passively and let the person beat me up, or I could fight back with the same violence they offered me. Through Jesus' words and example, however, I've found there's a third way that allows me to keep my dignity as a human being but doesn't compromise my morals by fighting back—like I did when I killed a man and received a lifelong prison sentence."

Charlie continues, "You see, Kevin, Jesus fights for equality, justice, and humanity while his third-way response exposes a disjointed and violent culture. Jesus isn't asking us to just 'take it' (which is pacifism), but he also doesn't want us grabbing a sword and retaliating (which is violence). Our culture offers us only two ways—but Jesus' third way means we turn our oppressors' tactics on their heads whenever we take action like turning the other cheek, offering all that we have, and walking the extra mile. When we do this, their strategies lose their power, and our humanity is restored.

"You know how many movies have to do with a 'good guy' getting back at a 'bad guy' who's done some form of injustice? Well, these movies promote what I call redemptive violence—the myth that responding to violence with violence makes things right. But redemption means to rescue or reclaim—it has nothing to do with violence."

Charlie hoped he hadn't said too much. But he could tell Kevin was actively listening, even though he never made eye contact. This was the first time Kevin had ever heard anything like this. He was very intrigued with this myth of "redemptive violence," as Charlie called it. But he struggled to see Jesus' third way as a realistic response. It required forgiveness and humility, and Kevin wasn't ready to embrace that just yet.

## Follow-Up Questions

- Do you ever hold onto bitterness and try to do life alone?

- Do you have a "Charlie" in your life who you've rejected or who you've allowed to be a part of your life?

- What are our culture's options for responding to someone who hurts us?

- What would it look like to enact this third-way response?

- What move can you make that will remind others that you're human?

In the past month, Charlie hadn't brought up Jesus' third way a single time. Yet Kevin couldn't get it out of his mind. So much of what he knew about "Christians," the Bible, and the responses of Christians who supposedly believed in the Bible didn't fall in line with what he'd heard from Charlie. In fact, Kevin tracked down a Bible from the prison library and read through Jesus' life as described in the book of Matthew. He found himself inspired and drawn in by the words and actions of Jesus. There was something incredibly strong about his humility and service. Jesus never compromised his dignity, but he also didn't compromise the dignity of those around him—not even those who opposed him.

Kevin knew he'd never get out of prison after killing Cory, but he nevertheless made the conscious decision to follow in the way of Jesus. And it was time for Kevin to get creative in responding to those who hoped to hurt him. He wanted to be known for his ability to humbly forgive rather than violently respond. Kevin decided that if his personal realignment in the way of Jesus was going to impact the world around him, then it must start with healing in his family.

For almost two years, Kevin had chosen anger and bitterness toward his parents for the way they'd raised him. He'd wanted nothing to do with them. His mother wrote him letters every week, but Kevin had mustered up the courage to read only a few of them. But after weeks of excited, hopeful discussion with Charlie about this new life in the way of Jesus, Charlie challenged Kevin to read his mother's letters and find a time to have a conversation with her.

With trembling fingers, he slowly ripped open the envelope containing his mother's most recent note. Kevin's heart skipped a beat as he read that his mother was planning to see him the *next day* in the hopes of talking with him. It was one thing for Kevin to begin the healing process with his parents by reading his mother's letters. But it was something else to see her in person. He suddenly couldn't read anymore, and he felt his stomach tighten. Kevin had carried so much pain and anger for so long. He wasn't sure how to live without it, and he certainly wasn't sure how to release it.

While lying on his bunk and staring up at the cement ceiling, Kevin was reminded of Jesus' words that followed the passage that Charlie had first introduced to him in Matthew 5:38–42. He opened his Bible to Matthew 5:43–48:

> You have heard that it was said, "Love your neighbor and hate your enemy." 44But I tell you: Love your enemies and pray for those who persecute you, 45that you may be sons of your Father in heaven. He causes his sun to rise on the evil and the good, and sends rain on the righteous and the unrighteous. 46If you love those who love you, what reward will you get? Are not even the tax collectors doing that? 47And if you greet only your brothers, what are you doing more than others? Do not even pagans do that? 48Be perfect, therefore, as your heavenly Father is perfect.

Reading these words didn't make the next step any easier or less painful. But again Kevin was inspired by the words of Jesus. Part of forgiving his mom meant loving her. As a follower of this radical way of life in Jesus, Kevin knew he had no other choice but to meet with his mother the next day.

After getting halfway to the meeting area and turning back to the safety of his cell, Kevin eventually built up the courage to turn around and walk toward his mother. He felt as though he were walking in a dream, and each step felt as though there were a ten-pound weight tied to his feet. After turning the final corner, he saw his mother sitting on the other side of thick glass and looking down into her purse. As she looked up, he sat down straight across from her. Both of their eyes filled with tears. She could sense that something profound had happened to her son, and he could see her love for him in her eyes.

In the twenty minutes they had together, they quickly shared stories and got caught up on the lives of family members. Kevin knew this wasn't the first time she'd come to see him, as the guards notified Kevin of her presence each month—he never chose to see his mom. She slowly looked down and then back up to meet Kevin's eyes. She said, "I've sat in this seat on the fourth Sunday of every month since you were put in prison. I knew you were probably angry with your father and me; we made so many mistakes. But I wanted you to know that I've always loved you, son." Kevin was saddened that his anger and bitterness kept him from reading her letters and spending time with her during her visits. He'd missed out on so much.

They only had a few minutes left, but Kevin could see some concern in his mother's eyes. She said, "Kevin, I have to tell you that the cousin of the boy you killed has been put into this same prison. I don't know anything else, but I'm sure he's angry with you. So please look out for yourself." Kevin's heart sank, and for a moment he was filled with fear. But just as quickly, he felt overcome by a spirit of peace. He told his mother he loved her and forgave her. They parted ways as both cried again, but this time they were tears of joy.

As the months passed, Kevin and Charlie became the best of friends. And Kevin established a reputation among the inmates and prison employees as a respected and honorable man. One of Kevin's favorite times of the day was when he'd walk around the back of the courtyard and feed the local stray dogs through the chain-link fence. Kevin would use the time by himself to think and pray while talking to the shaggy, four-legged creatures. He wasn't sure if anyone knew he went to this secluded spot, until one afternoon when he heard a low voice call out his name. Kevin spun around feeling startled. Standing there were three guys who didn't look all that happy. Kevin's heart dropped when he realized who the guy in the middle was—Cory's cousin.

The three backed Kevin up against the fence with the dogs yapping on the other side. Kevin could see that Cory's cousin had his hand wrapped tightly around some kind of sharp object. Stuck between panic and divine peace, Kevin could think only of Jesus' third way. Kevin had no desire to fight back and use violence to defend his cause, but he also didn't want to give in to the certain death these guys intended. Surprising even himself, Kevin began singing—loudly. One of his favorite bands was U2, so he sang, "It's a beautiful day . . ." It didn't take more than a couple of seconds until one of the guards heard the loud singing and looked around the corner to see Kevin and the three men. Cory's cousin hadn't drawn the weapon, so the three men just backed away as if nothing was going on. The guard walked closer to them.

Kevin couldn't help but smile. It was a nervous smile, but it was also a smile of hope—for a life that meant something. Kevin had been invited into the story of Jesus, and he couldn't wait to experience it every day.

## Follow-Up Discussion and Questions

- Recap the last three weeks on a whiteboard.

- Have teenagers pull out the main "nuggets" from each teaching and write them on the board.

- Break into small groups to discuss personal impact and application.

- Discuss the role of family in your life—how have you dealt with pain, hurt, and bitterness? Do you still have a lot of pain, hurt, and bitterness in your life? How do you respond to those who hurt you physically, emotionally, and verbally? In what ways have you been "taught" to respond? In what ways can you respond using this third way (or Jesus' Way) of retaliation? What examples in the world today show that we must either respond in a passive or violent way? What can we do to break that trend?

# 12

# JACOB
### *Topics—Dating Standards ("She Is HOT," "He Is POPULAR," etc.), Premarital Sex, Relationships, Trust*

Jacob never really thought much about his parents' divorce. He's now seventeen years old, and they've been divorced for three years. He has a few memories of his parents showing affection for each other, but most of his memories consist of long arguments and slammed doors. Maybe they got along better when he was really young, but he has no way of knowing. Besides, it doesn't matter anymore. Now that they're both single, they seem really happy to have their freedom.

Because his parents argued so much before the divorce, Jacob did his best to stay out of the house as much as possible. He had two best buddies growing up, Adam and Mark. They were twin brothers. The three of them could build forts out of mud and throw apples at cars for hours and hours. And whenever they came back to Adam and Mark's house to clean up and eat dinner, Jacob noticed something very different—he couldn't take his eyes off the connection between their parents. They'd make dinner together, and sometimes they'd even give each other hugs and say, "I love you." And it wasn't the obligatory "I love you"—it was for real. Jacob just figured they were weird. That certainly couldn't be what marriage was supposed to look like.

Being an only child and having observed his parents' marriage for years and years, Jacob decided the one thing he would NOT do was get married. His parents' new dating relationships looked pretty easy with their reduced commitment levels. For Jacob, relationships looked like fun, but marriage looked like the place where the fun ended. What's the point of being in a relationship that isn't fun, anyway?

It was with this mentality that Jacob, now a senior in high school, approached girls. They were objects of his fun, rather than people he was to serve before himself. He figured that if they didn't have anything to offer him (or he to them), it probably was best if they just didn't hang out. Now, Jacob did have standards and expectations for his dating relationships: Primarily, the girls had to be "hot."

Before they divorced, both of Jacob's parents had sex with other people. He can remember his dad once saying—in the middle of one of the *many* arguments he had with Jacob's mom—that "Being with her was the most freeing experience of my life!" In the end both parents went back to their lovers, so Jacob figured physical attraction should be the number-one priority in dating standards.

Jacob seemed to find girls with standards similar to his. Most often they were drawn to Jacob because he was popular. They figured that if they were with him, they'd gain self-worth and popularity. Jacob knew that was the reason the girls liked him, and he was just fine with that. As long as they both knew why they were in the relationship, he figured it would all work itself out.

Something interesting started to happen, though. As he dated these girls and had sex with them, the girls suddenly wanted more from him. He wasn't sure why; but after they had sex, there quickly became "more" to their connection. It was as if something had been purchased, and he couldn't just take it back and exchange it for something else. Jacob was just looking for fun and entertaining relationships, not heartfelt commitment.

After a few relationships ended at Jacob's initiative, he began to get a reputation as a heartbreaker. He thought, *Why do these girls take this so seriously? Don't we both just want to have fun?* This relational connection that these girls were so focused on after having sex with Jacob made him more confused and fearful of relationships than ever before.

For the first time in his life, Jacob began to wonder if he was taking a poor approach to relationships. He still didn't think relationships were inherently bad, but he knew he was missing something.

*(Note: This may be a good place to stop and have conversation. It also may be worthwhile to add more details to this first part of the story based on the dating dynamics of your audience.)*

Jacob was confused and appeared to be in deep thought most of the time. In fact, he'd often go to a café after school instead of hanging out with his friends, just so he could think: *Why do the girls I date expect so much more after we have sex? I mean, what else is supposed to be involved in having a relationship?* Jacob began to wonder if he'd missed something. He thought, *Could I just be a shallow, empty guy who's taking advantage of these girls? That certainly wasn't my intention; this is all I've ever known about relationships.*

One afternoon, the café was really crowded, and an older fellow asked if he could share Jacob's table. Jacob was deep in thought and was mildly startled by the request, but he welcomed the man to join him. At first it was really awkward sitting directly across from someone he didn't know, but soon they introduced themselves. The man's name was Jim, and he had a graying beard and a big smile. They began talking about sports and the weather, and soon Jim asked Jacob about his family. Again, Jacob felt a bit taken aback, but since he felt pretty comfortable talking with Jim, he began sharing. After about thirty minutes, Jacob realized he was running late for a dentist appointment and quickly said goodbye and left. But Jacob was intrigued by Jim, and he was disappointed that he hadn't been able to hear much of his story.

The next day at school, a girl that Jacob would normally have been very attracted to asked him if he wanted to go see a movie later that day. Usually, Jacob would say yes without thinking twice about it. But after his recent relational struggles, he took a few seconds to respond. To his own surprise—and in a sort of out-of-body experience—he told the girl he couldn't because he was meeting someone that afternoon at the local café. She seemed a little hurt and even more surprised by Jacob's response and quickly walked away. *What's wrong with me?* Jacob wondered.

He went back to the same table at the same time, hoping he might run into Jim. Jacob had never really had a conversation with an older man before. His dad was the closest thing to a mentor that Jacob had, and he never said much. After about five minutes, Jim walked in the door and gave Jacob a friendly grin before ordering his coffee. The older gentleman asked if he could sit with Jacob again and then sat down. Jacob quickly apologized for leaving so abruptly the day before and told Jim that he'd love to hear about his family.

Jim smiled and after taking a sip of his coffee, he said, "My wife is the best thing that ever happened to me. For some reason we've never been able to have kids, but we've had each other since we were twenty-two years old. Jacob, I'm sure this is hard for you to imagine, but we'll have been married forty years by the end of this year!" Jacob smiled but was confused. Jim's lighthearted grin and loving words about marriage didn't reflect the kind of marriage he'd known all his life.

Jim continued, "Son, it's been through my marriage that I've learned the most about myself. In fact, I can see my relationship with God most clearly through the lens of my relationship with my wife." Jacob wasn't sure what that meant. He'd never really thought much about God, especially in comparison to a relationship. Before Jacob could finish his thought, Jim continued, "I believe that any relationship must be defined by how willing you are to die for the other person. If I can't commit to this, then I don't deserve to be in that relationship. Why should my wife give all that she has to me if I'm not willing to give all that I have to her?"

This was almost too much for Jacob to take in. There was silence between them for the next couple of minutes, but it wasn't awkward. Jim could tell that Jacob was really wrestling with something, but he didn't want to push too hard. They spent the next five minutes talking about Jacob's hobbies and parted ways with a smile and a handshake. Jacob had a lot to think about.

After school the next day, Jacob drove to the café and parked in the lot again. But for some reason, he was nervous about talking with Jim today. He really hadn't had time to process all that was said yesterday, and he wasn't sure what to think. With some hesitation, Jacob drove away and went to another favorite thinking spot. It was a small pond surrounded by oak trees with a flat stump at the very end of a shallow cove. The trees were slightly blowing in the breeze, the birds were singing their songs, and every once in a while a bluegill or bass would slap the surface of the water while chasing an insect.

Jacob kept repeating in his head what Jim had said yesterday. *Why should my wife give all that she has to me if I'm not willing to give all that I have to her?* Jacob couldn't help but apply this to his dating relationships. *Those girls gave me everything they had when they had sex with me, and I wasn't willing to give all that I had back to them,* he thought. *That's why they feel so much more connected to me after we have sex!* There must have been something deeper going on. Jacob couldn't help but realize that he'd adopted a very shallow view of relationships. He could blame it all on his parents' example, but Jacob knew it was time for him to take responsibility for himself.

Jacob began to reflect on the one healthy relationship that seemed so "weird" to him growing up—the marriage of his best buddies' parents. Could that have been the type of relationship Jim spoke of? One that involved shared commitment in all aspects of life? Jacob began to realize that relationships involved a lot more than sex. So . . . had Jacob ever experienced a *real* relationship? He began to feel very lonely, but something in his spirit felt a bit more complete. He needed to talk to Jim.

The next day he waited for twenty minutes at the café until Jim finally walked through the door. Jacob had already bought a cup of coffee for Jim and had it waiting on the table. Jim offered Jacob his usual relaxed grin and firm handshake. Before Jim could say a word, Jacob began to unleash all the thoughts and realizations that had been flooding his mind and heart. Jim simply listened but inside he was jumping up and down at the growth of his young friend. He thought to himself, *I wonder if this is what it'd be like to have a son?* For now, to Jim, Jacob *was* his son.

Over the course of the next two weeks, Jim and Jacob met over coffee most every day. Jacob was learning what it meant to selflessly care for another individual, and Jim was enjoying the beauty of shared life and conversation. For the first time in his young life, Jacob decided to set up some relational standards other than his partner simply being "hot." What they could offer him was no longer a factor; instead it was what kind of commitment *he* could offer. Was he willing to die for that person?

The more Jacob wrestled with how he'd treated girls in the past, the more he realized the pain and hurt he'd caused them. He'd become overwhelmed with regret. But Jim gave him an idea for dealing with his regret—a way to symbolize "releasing" the pain he caused while initiating his new view of relationships. But it took Jacob quite a long time before he was ready—it was unlike anything he'd ever done before.

Then one day Jacob filled his car with helium balloons and headed down to his favorite spot by the pond. Carrying a handful of inflated balloons, Jacob walked around the pond to the shallow cove. As he sat on the stump, he took a deep breath and released one balloon. Then he took another deep breath and released another balloon. For Jacob, each balloon represented a regret that he was releasing to the heavens. As he exhaled, he visualized the separation he was making with his old self. With each inhale he pictured breathing in hope and a new way of viewing life.

As he continued this symbolic action, he felt as though there was something bigger going on. He thought, *Maybe the relationships I have now will have a direct effect on the relationships I'll have down the road. Maybe my relationships have an effect on my connection to a higher being? Jim mentioned that he grew closer to God through his relationship with his wife—are relationships that sacred?*

Jacob wasn't forgetting his regrets, but he was releasing them so he could view relationships in this more holistic way. He's not sure he'll ever be able to meet this higher standard, but Jacob plans on doing anything he can to meet it. He's willing to die for it.

(Note: The content of this story is driven by the follow-up conversations.)

- We are ALL worth dying for, and we must not believe anything else.
- When we date people, we shouldn't put ourselves at risk of entering sexual relationships; instead, we should pursue God's blessing in all things (*Shekinah*).
- Read "dating" example from *Sex God*, pages 126–27 and discuss.

Set Your Standards

- Christ-follower
- Same beliefs on dating, sex, and love
- Personality
- Parents' approval
- Similar interests

# APPENDICES

# Teaching through Story Basics

At every point in our story-creation process we need consider our own students' stories and the issues they face.

## Topic

- Should be an issue you've explored or are exploring
- Ask students questions
- Reflect on past conversations and experiences with students
- Research, research, research

## Basic Outline

- Come up with a skeleton story
- Main setting, characters, conflicts, climax, resolutions, Scripture

## Setting

- Basing it on personal experience can be effective (allows for added detail)
- Create a realistic location based on your cultural nuances
- Use a place that the students have experienced so they can visualize it

## Characters

- Main character: The character you're telling the story THROUGH. This person is central to most every aspect of your story (set-up, conflicts, climax, and resolution). Must develop Main Character very thoroughly and assign him/her believable attributes and character traits.
- Supporting character: Contributes to Main Character's story, whether for good or bad (protagonist/antagonist).
- Fringe characters: Lend credibility, understanding, and relevance to your story

146

## Plot Details

- Begin to get specific! Go back to your "skeleton" and manuscript each step the Main Character takes towards resolution. Bullet points may work as well. Write down everything, even if it sounds irrelevant at the moment. You can always go back and edit.

- Add content: Make sure your plot is at every point leading toward your main point/topic. Make sure it's backed with Scripture and theologically clear.

## Delivery

- Believe in the effectiveness of your story! (i.e., Don't say to your audience, "This is dumb!" or "I don't know what I was thinking!" etc.)

- Tell it like you were/are there; this adds excitement and detail

- Leave room for creativity

- Don't stress out if you miss a point

# Skeleton Story

**Topic:** Repenting to a Life Lived in the Kingdom of God – Participating in God's Story

**Setting:** California Bay area, present day, small-town neighborhood outside larger city

**Characters:** Jimmy, David, Henry (Recycle Can Guy), Jimmy and David's Friends, Parents, and Siblings

**Scripture Passage(s):** Matthew 3:2, 4:17, 5:3-10, 6:10, 19:21, 25:35-36, Mark 10:21, Life of Jesus in book of John & John 8:1-11, Philippians 2:1-4

## Plot:

- David and Jimmy are born into comfortable "Christian" homes
- They become close friends
- Life revolves around them
- They make fun of "Recycle Can Guy" on side of road whenever they ride their bikes by him
- Jimmy's grandma dies and writes him powerful letter that encourages him to live like Jesus
- Jimmy's forced to ask if there's more to life than simply playing video games and getting in trouble
- David is also impacted by Jimmy's story, and together they study the radical story of Jesus
- They realize that God's Story has been told for thousands of years THROUGH his people
- They choose to participate in God's continuing Story by living like Jesus
- They become friends with Recycle Can Guy, hear his story, and learn that his name is Henry
- Jimmy and David share Jesus with Henry through their acts of love, service, and caring conversation
- Henry gets very sick and dies, but not before experiencing the living God through Jimmy and David
- 30 years later the boys reflect on this being the time that their stories joined with God's Story

# Setting

**Primary Setting:** California Bay Area (Write a one- or two-word description of the primary setting)

## Characteristics:

- Closely connected neighborhood outside city
- Warm summer days, cold and foggy winter afternoons
- The boys (main characters) live near each other in a cul-de-sac
- Middle-class demographic
- Comfortable "American Dream" dynamics

## Personal Details:

- Local shopping center that is the "hang out"
- Not much to do, so they have to create own fun (i.e., throwing apples at cars, making fishing ponds, etc.)
- Ride bikes everywhere

## Alternate Settings: (Locations other than Primary Setting. If you want to get really detailed, you could make a similar sheet for each of them.)

- Henry's underground apartment
- Local cafe

*Remember: You're still picturing the faces and stories of your students!*

# Main Character

**Name:** Jimmy

## Main message(s) conveyed:

- It's easy to comfortably live a life centered around self
- Often it takes questioning and/or painful experiences to shake us out of our spiritual apathy so we realize we're created to participate in a Story much bigger than our own
- Shared mission, friendship, partnership, and accountability are essential to living as participants in God's redemptive and restorative Story
- Repenting (i.e., turning) from lives that ONLY serve our own stories toward lives that partner in God's Story brings fulfillment and purpose not only to us but also to the world

## Characteristics:

- Annoying younger brother to Sarah
- Disconnected son/grandson from his mother/father/grandma
- Athletic
- Outgoing with lots of friends
- Will do anything to impress other people
- Life revolves around him

## Interests:

- Sports (basketball, baseball, bike riding)
- Video games
- Hanging out with as many friends as possible, as often as possible

## Background:

- Raised in "Christian" home

- Heard about God and Jesus but never actually wrestled with how that applied to his life

- Had all the correct answers to spiritual questions, so his teachers and parents thought he "had it all together"

# Supporting Character #1

**Name:** David

## Main message(s) conveyed:
- There's power in an invitation to be in relationship with Jesus and partner in God's Story

- Friendship and shared vision for a new way of life in God's Kingdom is essential to spiritual growth

- It's often easy to be "friends" but not be in authentic relationships with those "friends"

## Characteristics:
- Follows the crowd and lacks self-esteem

- Unsure of himself in relation to friends/God

- Always up for an adventure

## Interests:
- Video games

- Baseball cards

- Sci-Fi-ish movies: *Star Wars*, *Lord of the Rings*, *Harry Potter*, etc.

## Background:
- Wealthy family
- Only went to church on major holidays growing up and sometimes with Jimmy

# Supporting Character #2

**Name:** Henry

## Main message(s) conveyed:
- Every person deserves our time, energy, and love
- If we simply take the time to hear someone's story, we'll find there's much more there than meets the eye
- Being participants in God's Story requires us to serve the Henrys of the world
- Simple acts of love can illuminate Jesus' redemptive and restorative message to the world around us

## Characteristics:
- Depressed and alone
- Lives in small storage closet under old apartment complex
- Addicted to drugs but hates himself for his addiction

## Interests:
- Collects cans and bottles and recycles them for drug money. Extra money is for food.
- Has family but at this point can only dream of their times together

## Background:

- Abandoned by all friends

- After his wife died 20 years earlier, Henry's daughter also abandoned him

- Used to be a factory worker, but after his wife's death Henry became depressed and turned to drugs

- Attended many recovery programs but felt like just another number

- Never met any self-proclaimed Christians who actually behaved like Jesus

# Fringe Characters

- Give them strategic roles that enhance your story's richness

| Name | Primary Role |
|---|---|
| Sarah | Jimmy's older sister who's often the recipient of his childish/selfish actions |
| Jimmy's mom | Prophetic voice calling Jimmy from his apathetic life toward one that cares for others. In the end chooses to partner with Jimmy and David in serving Henry |
| Jimmy's dad | Supports the family in every situation as Grandma gets sicker. Also chooses to support and partner with Jimmy and David in serving Henry |
| David's parents | Encourage David and Jimmy's new way of living by helping out with Henry |
| Jimmy and David's friends | Teenagers who reinforce the notion of self-focused lives and who need to be partners in God's Story |

# Story Plot

## Manuscript:

Write a comprehensive manuscript of your story from start to finish. You may want to break it up according to scene so it's easier to visualize each transition. This will also help with clarity when delivering the story. Giving each scene a title can also be a great way to visualize the direction of your story.

## Scene # 1: What a Life!

Jimmy and David were best of friends. They grew up living on the same street at the end of a cul-de-sac. Their very nice town was full of people who looked a lot like them and knew everyone else's names.

## Scene # 2: Grandma's Death

Soon after the boys turned 16 years old, Jimmy's grandmother grew ill. Jimmy wasn't sure why she was sick and didn't make an effort to connect with her—but Jimmy's mother did.

## Scene # 3: Painful Reflection

Jimmy could tell from the moment he saw his mother's somber face that she had something serious to share. "What is it, Mom?" he asked.

## Scene # 4: Exploring a New Kingdom

The next day David gave Jimmy his usual call to see if he wanted to get together and play some video games or ride bikes down to the shopping center. But after Jimmy read his grandmother's letter the day before and now hearing David's invitation to do the very things that took the place of spending time with his grandma, Jimmy felt sick...

## Scene # 5: A New Kind of Friendship

After a week David began to worry about his best buddy Jimmy, so David went over to Jimmy's house to see how he was doing. As soon as Jimmy opened the front door after David's knocks (David usually just walked in, but the door was locked this time), David could tell that Jimmy wasn't the same.

## Scene # 6: New Eyes: Participating in the Kingdom of God

Over the course of the next week, Jimmy began to hang out with his friends again. But now he viewed their actions and activities with new eyes. Jimmy was no longer content with how they'd been living and behaving for so long...

## Scene # 7 The Life of a Revolutionary

Jimmy guided David to the book of John where Jimmy had recently discovered how incredibly radical this guy Jesus was. They studied Jesus' life and then flipped back to the book of Matthew and studied the long invitation to a new way of living that Jesus offered his followers—the Sermon on the Mount.

# Teaching Outline (partial)

## Scene # 1: What a Life!

- Wild boys who grew up together and created a lot of havoc
- Every day after school they walked or rode bikes down to the shopping center (every day during the summer)
- They saw an older man collecting cans and walking slowly on their path nearly every day
- They made fun of him constantly
- Life was all about Jimmy and David, how to have the most fun (i.e., hanging at friends' houses, watching movies, all-nighters, etc.)
- They weren't "bad" boys, but everything had to cater to them

## Scene # 2: Grandma's Death

- When Jimmy and David were 16, Jimmy's grandma grew very ill. Jimmy didn't know her that well, but she lived close by
- Jimmy's mom encouraged Jimmy to spend time with his grandma, but he never make the time
- Jimmy never thought his grandma would actually die, so he just kept living his Jimmy-centered life
- Grandma died a slow, painful death; Jimmy was not greatly affected until...

## Scene # 3: Painful Reflection

- Jimmy received a letter his grandma had written to him shortly before she died
- (Leader/Teacher: Read letter out loud to group)
- Jimmy broke down and began to reflect on his life and how little of it he'd spent serving/loving
- Jimmy did very little of either...especially to those who didn't fit into his schedule

## Share Your Thoughts

**With the Author:** Your comments will be forwarded to
the author when you send them to *zauthor@zondervan.com.*

**With Zondervan:** Submit your review of this book
by writing to *zreview@zondervan.com.*

## Free Online Resources at
## www.zondervan.com

**Zondervan AuthorTracker:** Be notified whenever your favorite
authors publish new books, go on tour, or post an update
about what's happening in their lives at www.zondervan.com/
authortracker.

**Daily Bible Verses and Devotions:** Enrich your life with daily
Bible verses or devotions that help you start every morning
focused on God. Visit www.zondervan.com/newsletters.

**Free Email Publications:** Sign up for newsletters on Christian
living, academic resources, church ministry, fiction, children's
resources, and more. Visit www.zondervan.com/newsletters.

**Zondervan Bible Search:** Find and compare Bible passages in
a variety of translations at www.zondervanbiblesearch.com.

**Other Benefits:** Register yourself to receive online benefits
like coupons and special offers, or to participate in research.

ZONDERVAN®

ZONDERVAN.com/
AUTHORTRACKER
*follow your favorite authors*

CPSIA information can be obtained at www.ICGtesting.com
Printed in the USA
LVOW09s1002140314

377429LV00003B/3/P